Learning Hunk

Visualize and analyze your Hadoop data using Hunk

Dmitry Anoshin

Sergey Sheypak

BIRMINGHAM - MUMBAI

Learning Hunk

First published: December 2015

Production reference: 1181215

Published by Packt Publishing Ltd.
Livery Place
35 Livery Street
Birmingham B3 2PB, UK.

ISBN 978-1-78217-482-0

www.packtpub.com

Credits

Authors
Dmitry Anoshin

Sergey Sheypak

Reviewers
Jigar Bhatt

Neil Mehta

Acquisition Editors
Hemal Desai

Reshma Raman

Content Development Editor
Anish Sukumaran

Technical Editor
Shivani Kiran Mistry

Copy Editor
Stephen Copestake

Project Coordinator
Izzat Contractor

Proofreader
Safis Editing

Indexer
Hemangini Bari

Graphics
Jason Monteiro

Production Coordinator
Nilesh Mohite

Cover Work
Nilesh Mohite

About the Authors

Dmitry Anoshin is a data-centric technologist and a recognized expert in building and implementing big data and analytics solutions. He has a successful track record when it comes to implementing business and digital intelligence projects in numerous industries, including retail, finance, marketing, and e-commerce.

Dmitry possesses in-depth knowledge of digital/business intelligence, ETL, data warehousing, and big data technologies. He has extensive experience in the data integration process and is proficient in using various data warehousing methodologies. Dmitry has constantly exceeded project expectations when he has worked for financial, machine tool, and retail industries.

He has completed a number of multinational full BI/DI solution life cycle implementation projects. With expertise in data modeling, Dmitry also has a background and business experience in multiple relation databases, OLAP systems, and NoSQL databases.

In addition, he has reviewed *SAP BusinessObjects Reporting Cookbook*, *Creating Universes with SAP BusinessObjects*, and *Learning SAP BusinessObjects Dashboards*, all by Packt Publishing and was the author of *SAP Lumira Essentials*, *Packt Publishing*.

I would like to tell my wife Sveta how much I love her. I dedicate this book to my wife and children, Vasily and Anna. Thank you for your never-ending support that keeps me going.

Sergey Sheypak started his so-called big data practice in 2010 as a Teradata PS consultant. His was leading the Teradata Master Data Management deployment in Sberbank, Russia (which has 110 billion customers). Later Sergey switched to AsterData and Hadoop practices. Sergey joined the Research and Development team at MegaFon (one of the top three telecom companies in Russia with 70 billion customers) in 2012. While leading the Hadoop team at MegaFon, Sergey built ETL processes from existing Oracle DWH to HDFS. Automated end-to-end tests and acceptance tests were introduced as a mandatory part of the Hadoop development process. Scoring geospatial analysis systems based on specific telecom data were developed and launched. Now, Sergey works as independent consultant in Sweden.

About the Reviewer

Jigar Bhatt is a computer engineering undergraduate from the National Institute of Technology, Surat. He specializes in big data technologies and has a deep interest in data science and machine learning. He has also engineered several cloud-based Android applications. He is currently working as a full-time software developer at a renowned start-up, focusing on building and optimizing cloud platforms and ensuring profitable business intelligence round the clock.

Apart from academics, he finds adventurous sports enthralling. He can be reached at http://www.jigarbhatt.in/.

> I would like to thank Dr. Dhiren Patel from the computer engineering department, NIT, Surat, who encouraged my interest in data science and guided me through the initial stages of building my career in the big data world.

Neil Mehta BSc (Hons) has 20 years of experience as a developer, analyst, and program manager and has spent the last 7 years specifically implementing business intelligence solutions to help companies leverage their corporate data. Trained in all aspects of analytics from data modeling to system architecture and reporting, Neil currently manages a large team of data architects, ETL developers, and report designers for a large insurance company.He has extensive experience with business analytics, administration, and dashboard design and has helped develop programs to establish super user communities and develop training plans. He has worked in multiple business segments, including financial, oil and gas, transportation, and retail industries.

www.PacktPub.com

Support files, eBooks, discount offers, and more

For support files and downloads related to your book, please visit www.PacktPub.com.

Did you know that Packt offers eBook versions of every book published, with PDF and ePub files available? You can upgrade to the eBook version at www.PacktPub.com and as a print book customer, you are entitled to a discount on the eBook copy. Get in touch with us at service@packtpub.com for more details.

At www.PacktPub.com, you can also read a collection of free technical articles, sign up for a range of free newsletters and receive exclusive discounts and offers on Packt books and eBooks.

https://www2.packtpub.com/books/subscription/packtlib

Do you need instant solutions to your IT questions? PacktLib is Packt's online digital book library. Here, you can search, access, and read Packt's entire library of books.

Why subscribe?

- Fully searchable across every book published by Packt
- Copy and paste, print, and bookmark content
- On demand and accessible via a web browser

Free access for Packt account holders

If you have an account with Packt at www.PacktPub.com, you can use this to access PacktLib today and view 9 entirely free books. Simply use your login credentials for immediate access.

Table of Contents

Preface

This book offers a step-by-step approach to learning Hunk, diving into the technical aspects of it first. It will demonstrate the various aspects of big data analytics using the powerful capabilities of Hunk. In addition to this, it provides detailed sections on the deployment and configuration of Hunk on top of Hadoop and the NoSQL data stores. It will also teach you how to create queries using SPL, reports, and dashboards. This book covers security questions and demonstrates how to set up security for big data implementation based on Hadoop and Hunk. Moreover, it will teach you how to use the Hunk SDK and extend its default functionality. Finally, it acts as a guide to deploying Hunk on top of MongoDB and AWS Elastic MapReduce.

What this book covers

Chapter 1, *Meet Hunk*, covers Hunk and its basic features. Hunk is a full-featured platform to rapidly explore, analyze, and visualize data in Hadoop and the NoSQL data stores. You will learn how to install and configure Hunk. Moreover, you will learn about Hunk's architecture and Hunk Virtual Index. You will also be introduced to loading data into Hadoop in order to aid its discovery by Hunk.

Chapter 2, *Explore Hadoop Data with Hunk*, talks about how you can easily analyze and visualize data using the Splunk search processing language (SPL). Getting a large amount of data into Hadoop is easy but getting analytics from this data is the challenge. You will learn about the use cases of big data analytics and the security aspect of Hunk.

Chapter 3, *Meet Hunk Features*, teaches you about Hunk's knowledge objects. Hunk is a powerful big data analytics platform, which gives us many tools in order to explore, analyze, and visualize big data. You will learn how to build a semantic layer on top of Hadoop and discover data using the friendly user interface of Hunk Pivot.

Chapter 4, *Adding Speed to Reports*, covers the techniques related to report acceleration. Hunk is an extremely powerful tool and can handle a vast amount of data. However, business decisions, which depend on fresh data, can't wait.

Chapter 5, *Customizing Hunk*, introduces REST API, SDK, and so on. Sometimes, we want to get out of the box or need to meet business expectations and are restricted by the initial functionality. Thus, you will learn how to create customized visualization, and you will also be introduced to the Splunk Web Framework.

Chapter 6, *Discovering Hunk Integration Apps*, introduces you to Hunk's apps that can easily integrate with the NoSQL data stores, such as MongoDB or Sqqrl. Hunk is a universal big data analytics platform, which can easy explore data in Hadoop or the NoSQL data stores. You will learn how to connect MongoDB and explore data in its data store.

Chapter 7, *Exploring Data in the Cloud*, shows you how to analyze data in AWS Cloud. Some big organizations prefer to store their big data on the cloud because it gives them many benefits.

What you need for this book

In this book, you will learn how to explore, analyze, and visualize big data in Hadoop or the NoSQL data stores with the powerful, full-featured big data analytics platform, Hunk. You will discover real-world examples, dive into Hunk's architecture and capabilities, as well as learn how to build Operation Intelligence using this technology. Additionally, you will learn about report acceleration techniques, data models, and custom dashboards and views using Hunk. Moreover, this book focuses on popular use cases using powerful Hunk apps, which provide integration with the NoSQL data stores and give complete visibility into your end-to-end big data operations. Finally, you will about the Splunk web framework. We just require a laptop or PC with a 4 GB RAM (8 GB RAM recommended) and VirtualBox installed. There aren't any specific hardware requirements as VirtualBox should work everywhere.

Who this book is for

If you are big data enthusiast and want to get more business insight and build efficient, real-time Operation Intelligence Solution based on Hadoop deployments or various NoSQL data stores using Hunk, this book is for you. Aimed on big data developers, managers and consultants this is also a comprehensive reference for everyone, who want to learn how to analyze and explore big data with one of the most powerful and flexible big data analytics platform.

Conventions

In this book, you will find a number of text styles that distinguish between different kinds of information. Here are some examples of these styles and an explanation of their meaning.

Code words in text, database table names, folder names, filenames, file extensions, pathnames, dummy URLs, user input, and Twitter handles are shown as follows: "Rename the count field as qty."

A block of code is set as follows:

```
<property>
    <name>dfs.permissions.enabled</name>
    <value>true</value>
</property>
<property>
    <name>dfs.permissions</name>
    <value>true</value>
</property>
<property>
    <name>hadoop.proxyuser.root.hosts</name>
    <value>*</value>
</property>
<property>
    <name>hadoop.proxyuser.root.groups</name>
    <value>*</value>
</property>
```

Any command-line input or output is written as follows:

```
[cloudera@quickstart ~]$ whoami
cloudera
[cloudera@quickstart ~]$ sudo su
[root@quickstart cloudera]# whoami
root
[root@quickstart cloudera]#
```

New terms and **important words** are shown in bold. Words that you see on the screen, for example, in menus or dialog boxes, appear in the text like this: "Go to menu **Machine** | **Add** and point to the extracted VBOX file."

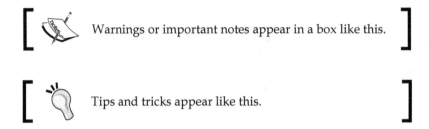

> Warnings or important notes appear in a box like this.

> Tips and tricks appear like this.

Reader feedback

Feedback from our readers is always welcome. Let us know what you think about this book—what you liked or disliked. Reader feedback is important for us as it helps us develop titles that you will really get the most out of.

To send us general feedback, simply e-mail feedback@packtpub.com, and mention the book's title in the subject of your message.

If there is a topic that you have expertise in and you are interested in either writing or contributing to a book, see our author guide at www.packtpub.com/authors.

Customer support

Now that you are the proud owner of a Packt book, we have a number of things to help you to get the most from your purchase.

Downloading the example code

You can download the example code files from http://www.bigdatapath.com/wp-content/uploads/2015/05/learning-hunk-05-with-mongo.zip.

Downloading the color images of this book

We also provide you with a PDF file that has color images of the screenshots/diagrams used in this book. The color images will help you better understand the changes in the output. You can download this file from http://www.packtpub.com/sites/default/files/downloads/LearningHunk_ColorImages.pdf.

Errata

Although we have taken every care to ensure the accuracy of our content, mistakes do happen. If you find a mistake in one of our books—maybe a mistake in the text or the code—we would be grateful if you could report this to us. By doing so, you can save other readers from frustration and help us improve subsequent versions of this book. If you find any errata, please report them by visiting http://www.packtpub.com/submit-errata, selecting your book, clicking on the **Errata Submission Form** link, and entering the details of your errata. Once your errata are verified, your submission will be accepted and the errata will be uploaded to our website or added to any list of existing errata under the Errata section of that title.

To view the previously submitted errata, go to https://www.packtpub.com/books/content/support and enter the name of the book in the search field. The required information will appear under the **Errata** section.

Piracy

Piracy of copyrighted material on the Internet is an ongoing problem across all media. At Packt, we take the protection of our copyright and licenses very seriously. If you come across any illegal copies of our works in any form on the Internet, please provide us with the location address or website name immediately so that we can pursue a remedy.

Please contact us at copyright@packtpub.com with a link to the suspected pirated material.

We appreciate your help in protecting our authors and our ability to bring you valuable content.

Questions

If you have a problem with any aspect of this book, you can contact us at questions@packtpub.com, and we will do our best to address the problem.

1
Meet Hunk

Before getting started with Hunk, let's dive into the problem of modern big data analytics and highlight the main drawbacks and challenges. It is important to understand how Hunk works and what goes on under the hood. In addition, we'll compare Splunk and Enterprise in order to understand their differences and what they have in common as powerful and flexible products. Finally, we'll perform a lot of practical exercises through real-world use cases.

In this chapter you will learn:

- What big data analytics is
- Big data challenges and the disadvantages of modern big data analytics tools
- Hunk's history
- Hunk's architecture
- How to set up Hadoop for Hunk
- Real-world use cases

Big data analytics

We are living in the century of information technology. There are a lot of electronic devices around us that generate lots of data. For example, you can surf the Internet, visit a couple of news portals, order new Nike Air Max shoes from a web store, write a couple of messages to your friends, and chat on Facebook. Every action produces data. And we can multiply the actions by the amount of people who have access to the Internet, or just use a mobile phone, and we get really **big data**. Of course, you have a question: how big is big data? It probably starts from terabytes or even petabytes now. The volume is not the only issue; we are also struggling with the *variety* of data. As a result, it is not enough to analyze just the data structure. We should explore unstructured data, such as machine data generated by various machines.

World-famous enterprises try to collect this extremely big data in order to monetize it and find business insights. Big data offers us new opportunities; for example, we can enrich customer data through social networks, using the APIs of Facebook or Twitter. We can build customer profiles and try to predict customer wishes in order to sell our product or improve the customer experience. It is easy to say, but difficult to do. However, organizations try to overcome these challenges and use big data stores, such as Hadoop.

The big problem

Hadoop is a distributed file system and a distributed framework designed to compute large chunks of data. It is relatively easy to get data into Hadoop. There are plenty of tools for getting data into different formats, such as Apache Phoenix. However it is actually extremely difficult to get value out of the data you put into Hadoop.

Let's look at the path from data to value. First we have to start with collecting data. Then we also spend a lot of time preparing it, making sure that this data is available for analysis, and being able to question the data. This process is as follows:

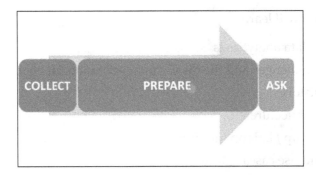

Unfortunately, you may not have asked the right questions or the answers are not clear, and you have to repeat this cycle. Maybe you have transformed and formatted your data. In other words, it is a long and challenging process.

What you actually want is to collect the data and spend some time preparing it; then you can ask questions and get answers repetitively. Now, you can spend a lot of time asking multiple questions. In addition, you can iterate with data on those questions to refine the answers that you are looking for. Let's look at the following diagram, in order to find a new approach:

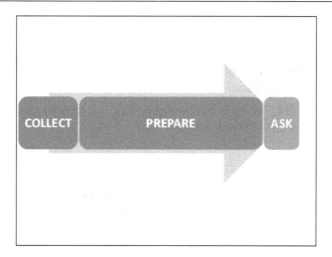

The elegant solution

What if we could take Splunk and put it on top of all the data stored in Hadoop? This is what Splunk actually did. The following shows the names Hunk was derived from:

Hadoop + Splunk = Hunk

Let's discuss some goals that Hunk's inventors were thinking about when they were planning Hunk:

- Splunk can take data from Hadoop via the Splunk Hadoop Connection App. However, it is a bad idea to copy massive amounts of data from Hadoop to Splunk, it is much better to process data in-place, because Hadoop provides both storage and computation; why not take advantage of both of them?

- Splunk has the extremely powerful **Splunk Processing Language** (**SPL**) and it has a wide range of analytic functions. That's why it is a good idea to keep SPL in the new product.

- Splunk has a true on-the-fly schema. Data that we store in Hadoop changes constantly. So, Hunk has to be able build a schema on-the-fly independently of the data format.

- It is a very good idea to provide the ability to make a preview. As you know, when searching you can get incremental results. It can dramatically reduce outage. For example, we don't want to wait till a map reduce job finishes; we can look at the incremental result and, in the event of a wrong result, we can restart the search query.

- Deployment of Hadoop is not easy, and Splunk tries to make the installation and configuration of Hunk easy for us.

Supporting SPL

Let's discuss more closely the reasons for supporting SPL. You are probably familiar with Splunk and SPL and know how powerful and flexible this language is. These are some of the advantages of SPL:

- Naturally suitable for `MapReduce`

- Reduces adoption time for people who are already familiar with Splunk

There are some challenges in integrating SPL and Hadoop. Hadoop is written in Java but all SPL code is in C++. Does SPL need to convert to Java or reuse what Splunk has provided? Finally, it was decided to reuse C++ code entirely.

Intermediate results

No one likes to look at a blank screen. A lot of people using other tools such as Pig or Hive have to wait until the query is finished and you have no idea what the query is actually retrieving for you. Maybe you made a mistake, but you didn't know about it; you will have to wait till the job is completed. It is a kind of frustration—running queries and waiting for hours.

That's why the Hunk team gave their users the ability to preview the result. You will be able to play with this in future chapters.

Getting to know Hunk

Before going deeper into Hunk, let's clarify what Hunk does not do:

- Hunk does not replace your Hadoop distribution

- Hunk does not replace or require Splunk Enterprise

- Interactive but no real-time or needle in the haystack searches

- No data ingest management

- No Hadoop operation management

Hunk is a full-featured platform for rapidly exploring, analyzing, and visualizing data in Hadoop and NoSQL data stores. Based on years of experience building big data products deployed to thousands of Splunk customers, Hunk drives dramatic improvements in the speed and simplicity of getting insights from raw, unstructured, or polystructured big data—all without building fixed schemas or moving data to a separate in-memory store. Hunk delivers proven value for security, risk management, product analytics, a 360-degree customer view, and the Internet of Things.

While many big data initiatives take months and have high rates of failure, Hunk offers a unique approach. Hunk provides a single, fluid user experience designed to drive rapid insights from your big data. Hunk empowers self-service analytics for anyone in your department or organization to quickly and easily unlock actionable insights from raw big data, wherever it may reside.

These are the main capabilities of Hunk:

- Full-featured, integrated analytics
- Fast to deploy and drive value
- Interactive search
- Supported data formats
- Report acceleration
- Results preview
- Drag-and-drop analytics
- Rich developer environment
- Custom dashboards and views
- Secure access
- Hunk apps
- Hunk on the AWS cloud

Splunk versus Hunk

Let's compare Splunk and Hunk:

Features	Splunk Enterprise	Hunk
Indexing	Native	Virtual
Where data is stored and read	Splunk Buckets on Local or SAN Disks	Any Hadoop-compatible file system (HDFS, MapR, Amazon S3) and NoSQL, or other data stores via streaming resource libraries
A 60-day free trial license	500 MB/day	Unlimited
Pricing model	Data invested per day	Number of task trackers (compute nodes in YARN)
Real-time streaming events	+	+
Data model	+	+
Pivot	+	+
Rich developer environment	+	+
Event breaking, timestamp extraction, source typing	+	+
Rare term search	Index time	Search time
Report acceleration	Fast: Uses index and bloom filters	Slow: Requires full data scan within partitions
Access control and single sign-on	+	+
Universal forwarder	+	NA
Forwarder management	+	NA
Splunk apps	+	Limited
Premium apps	+	N/A
Standard support	+	+
Enterprise support	+	+

In the preceding table + means product support mentioned feature and NA means feature is not supported in a product.

As you saw, there are some differences. But Hunk is designed for another purpose; it is a kind face in the complex world of big data. Throughout this book, we will introduce the various features of Hunk and you will definitely learn this amazing tool.

Let's look closely at Hunk and try to understand how it works.

Hunk architecture

Let's explore how Hunk looks. From the end user perspective, Hunk looks like Splunk. You use same interface, you can write searches, visualize big data, and create reports, dashboards, and alerts. In other words, Hunk can do everything Splunk can do. In the following screenshot, you can see a schematic of Hunk's architecture:

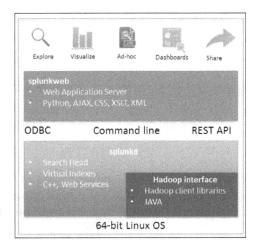

Hunk has the same interface and command lines as well. The only change is that Splunk works with data stored in native indexes but the Hunk SPL acts with external data; that's why they call virtual indexes.

Connecting to Hadoop

Hunk is designed to connect to Hadoop via the Hadoop interface. The following screenshot demonstrates that Hunk can connect a Hadoop cluster via Hadoop client libraries and Java:

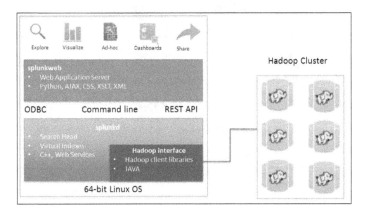

Moreover, Hunk can work with multiple Hadoop clusters:

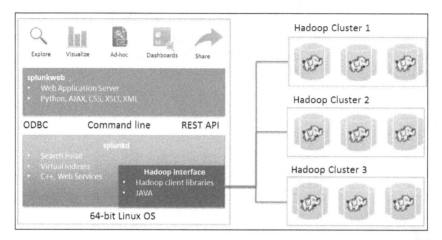

In addition, you can use Splunk and Hunk together. You can connect Splunk Enterprise if you have Splunk and Hadoop in your environment. As a result, it is possible to correlate Hunk searches through Hadoop and Splunk Enterprise via the same search head.

Advance Hunk deployment

Sometimes, organizations have really big data. They have thousands of instances of Hadoop. It is a real challenge to get business insight from this extremely large data. However, Hunk can easily handle this titanic task. Of course this isn't as easy as it sounds, but it is possible because you can scale Hunk deployments. Let's look at the following example:

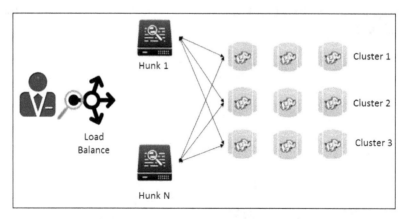

There are hundreds or thousands of users who put their business questions to big data. business users send their queries, they go through the **Load Balancer** (**LB**), LB sends them to Hunk, and Hunk makes distributive work to Hadoop.

Native versus virtual indexes

Before we start to compare native and virtual indexes, let's use our previous Splunk experience and see how SPL actually works.

For example, we have a query:

```
Index=main | stats count by status | rename count AS qty
```

As you may remember, every step in Splunk is divided by pipes. You can read expression from left to right and follow expression execution sequence.

 Splunk development was motivated by Unix Shell pipes.

In our example, we:

1. Get all data from `Index=main`.
2. Count all rows for every status.
3. Rename the `count` field as `qty`.
4. Retrieve the final result.

 It is interesting to know that SPL uses a `MapReduce` algorithm. In other words, it has a map phase when performing retrieve operations and reducing step, and when performing count operations.

The rule is that the first search command is always responsible for retrieving events.

Native indexes

Before Hunk was created, there were only the native indexes of Splunk Enterprise. The data was ingested by Splunk and access to it was via the Splunk interface.

A native index is basically a data store or collection of data. We can put web logs, syslogs, or other machine data in Splunk. We have access controls and the ability to give permissions to users to access data on specific indexes. In addition, Splunk gives us the opportunity to optimize popular and heavy searches. As a result, business users will get their dashboards very quickly.

Virtual index

Virtual indexes lack some features of native indexes. A virtual index is a data container with access controls. Hunk can only read data. Data gets into Hadoop somehow and Hunk can use this data as a container. The inventors of Hunk decided to not build indexes on top of Hadoop data and to not optimize Hunk to perform needle-in-the-haystack searches. However, if data layout is properly designed in Hadoop (for example, there is a hierarchical structure or data is organized based on the timestamp, year, month, or date), this can really improve search performance.

Let's compare both indexes in one table:

Native Indexes	Virtual Indexes
Serve as data containers	Serve as data containers
Access control	Access control
Reads/writes	Read only
Data retention policies	N/A
Optimized for keyword search	N/A
Optimized for time range search	Available via regex/pruning

 You can learn more about virtual indexes on the Splunk website: `http://docs.splunk.com/Documentation/Hunk/latest/Hunk/Virtualindexes`.

External result provider

The core technology of Hunk is a virtual index and **External Result Provider** (ERP). We have already encountered virtual indexes. The term ERP is sometime known as **resource provider**.

The ERP is basically a helper process. It goes out and deals with the details of the external systems that are going to interact with Hadoop or another data store. In other words, it takes searches that users perform in Hunk and somehow translates or interprets them in `mrjob`. That's how it pushes computation.

There are a few other implementations of ERP that Splunk's partners developed in order to integrate Hunk with Mongo DB, Apache Accumulo, and Cassandra. There are just different implementations of the same interface that helps Hunk to interact with external systems and use any type of data via virtual indexes.

The following diagram demonstrates how ERP looks:

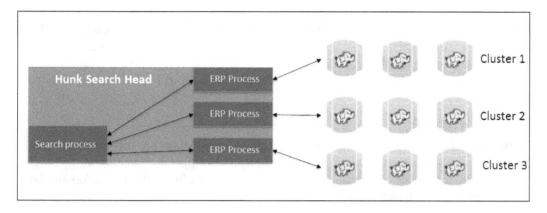

For each Hadoop cluster (or external system) the search process spawns an ERP process that is responsible for executing the (remote part of the) search on that system.

 You can learn more about ERP on the Splunk web site:
http://docs.splunk.com/Documentation/Hunk/
latest/Hunk/Externalresultsproviders.

Computation models

Previously, we considered some challenges in big data analytics and found out powerful solutions via Hunk. Now we can go deeper in order to understand some of the core advantages of Hunk. Let's start with an easy question: *how do we provide interactivity?*

There are at least two computational models.

Data streaming

In this approach, data moves from HDFS to the search head. In other words, data is processed in a streaming fashion. As a result users can immediately start to work with data, slice and dice it, or visualize when the first bytes of data will start to appear. But there is a problem with this process. It is a huge volume of data to move and process.

There is one primary benefit that you will probably get; there is a very low response time. In addition, we get low throughput that is not very positive for us.

Data reporting

The second mode is moving computation to data. The way to do this is to create and start a MapReduce job to do the processing, monitor the MapReduce job, and, finally, collect the results. Then, merge the results and visualize the data. There is another problem here—late feedback, because the MapReduce job might take a long time. As a result, this approach has high latency and high throughput.

Mixed mode

Both modes have their pros and cons, but the most important are low latency, because it gives interactivity, and high throughput, because it gives us the opportunity to process larger datasets. These are all benefits and Hunk takes the best from both computational modes.

Let's visualize both modes in order to better understand how they work:

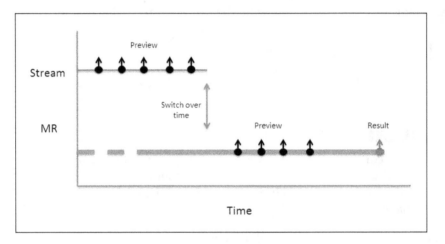

In addition, we consolidate all the modes in the following table, in order to make things clearer:

Streaming	Reporting	Mixed Mode
Pull data from HDFS to search head for processing	Push compute down to data and consume results	Start both streaming and reporting models. Show streaming results until reporting starts to complete
Low latency	High latency	Low latency
Low throughput	High throughput	High throughput

Hunk security

With version 6.1, Hunk became more secure. By default Hunk has superusers with full access. However, very often organizations want to apply a security model to their corporate data, in order to keep their data safe. Hunk can use pass-through authentication. It gives the opportunity to control how MapReduce jobs can submit users and what HDFS files they can access. In addition, it is possible to specify the queue MapReduce jobs should use.

Pass-through authentication gives us the capability to make the Hunk superuser a proxy for any number of configured Hunk users. As a result, Hunk users can act as Hadoop users to own the associated jobs, tasks, and files in Hadoop (and it can limit access to files in HDFS.). Let's look at the following diagram:

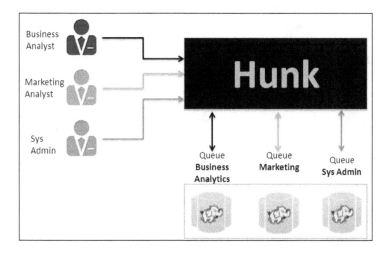

Let's explore some common use cases that can help us understand how it works.

One Hunk user to one Hadoop user

For example, say we want our Hunk user to act as a Hadoop user associated with a specific queue or data set. Then we just map the Hunk user to a specific user in Hadoop. For example, in Hunk the user name is Hemal, but in Hadoop it is HemalDesai and the queue is Books.

Many Hunk users to one Hadoop user

For example, say we have many Hunk users and want them to act as a Hadoop user. In Hunk, we can have several users such as Dmitry, Hemal, and Sergey, but in Hadoop they will all execute as an Executive user and will be assigned to the Books queue.

Hunk user(s) to the same Hadoop user with different queues

For example, say you have many Hunk users and the same Hadoop users; it is possible to assign them different queues.

Security will be discussed more closely in *Chapter 3, Meet Hunk Features*.

Setting up Hadoop

Before starting to play with Hadoop and Hunk, we are going to download and run a VM. You'll get a short description on how to get everything up and running and put in some data for processing later.

Starting and using a virtual machine with CDH5

We have decided to take the default Cloudera CDH 5.3.1 VM from the Cloudera site and fine-tune it for our needs. Please open this link to prepare a VM: http://www.bigdatapath.com/2015/08/learning-hunk-links-to-vm-with-all-stuff-you-need/.

This post may have been be updated by the time you're reading this book.

SSH user

You can run the terminal application by clicking the special icon on the top bar:

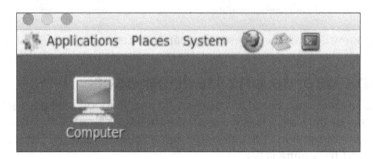

Your user is cloudera. sudo is passwordless:

```
[cloudera@quickstart ~]$ whoami
cloudera
[cloudera@quickstart ~]$ sudo su
[root@quickstart cloudera]# whoami
```

```
root
[root@quickstart cloudera]#
```

MySQL

MySQL is used as an example of the data ingestion process. The user name is dwhuser, the password is dwhuser. You can get root access by using the root username and the cloudera password:

```
[cloudera@quickstart ~]$ mysql -u root -p

mysql> show databases;
+--------------------+
| Database           |
+--------------------+
| information_schema |
| cdrdb              |
| cm                 |
| firehose           |
| hue                |
| metastore          |
| mysql              |
| oozie              |
| retail_db          |
| sentry             |
+--------------------+
10 rows in set (0.00 sec)
```

We import data from MySQL to Hadoop from the database named cdrdb. There are some other databases. They are used by Cloudera Manager services and Hadoop features such as Hive Metastore, Oozie, and so on.

Hive Metastore is a service designed to centralize metadata management. It's a kind of Teradata DBC.Table, DBC.Columns, or IBM DB2 syscat.Columns, syscat.Tables. The idea is to create a strict schema description over the bytes stored in Hadoop and then get access to this data using SQL.

Oozie is a kind of Hadoop CRON without **a Single Point of Failure (SPOF)**. Think it through; is it easy to create a distributed reliable CRON with failover functionality? Oozie uses RDBMS to persist metadata about planned, running, and finished tasks. This VM doesn't provide an Oozie HA configuration.

Starting the VM and cluster in VirtualBox

Perform the following steps:

1. Install VirtualBox: `https://www.virtualbox.org/`.

2. Follow the link and download the VM ZIP.

3. Extract the ZIP to your local drive.

4. Open VirtualBox.

5. Go to menu **Machine** | **Add** and point to the extracted VBOX file.

6. You should see the imported VM:

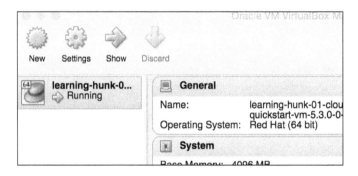

7. Run the imported VM.

Big data use case

We are going to use several data sources for our applications. The first will use RDBMS interaction since it's one of the most popular use cases. We will show you how to integrate *classical* data with a strict schema from the RDBMS small dictionary stored in HDFS. Data from RDBMS has *big* volume in real life (we just have a small subset of it now) and the dictionary keeps the dimensions for the RDBMS value. We will enrich the big data with the dimensions before displaying data on the map.

Importing data from RDBMS to Hadoop using Sqoop

There are many ways to import data into Hadoop; we could easily publish a book called "1,001 methods to put your data into Hadoop." We are not going to focus on these specialties and will use very simple cases. Why so simple? Because you will meet many problems in a production environment and we can't cover these in a book.

An example from real life: you will definitely need to import data from your existing DWH into Hadoop. And you will have to use Sqoop in conjunction with special Teradata/Oracle connectors to do it quickly without DWH performance penalties. You will spend some time tuning your DB storage schema and connection properties to achieve a reasonable result. That is why we decided to keep all this tricky stuff out of the book; our goal is to use Hunk on top of Hadoop.

Here is a short explanation of the import process. We've split the diagram into three parts:

- MySQL, a database that stores data
- Oozie, responsible for triggering the job import process
- Hadoop, responsible for getting data from MySQL DB and storing it in an HDFS catalog

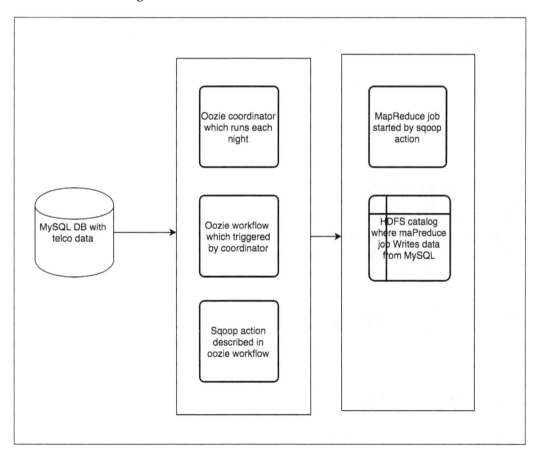

Initially, the data is stored in MySQL DB. We want to copy the data to HDFS for later processing using Hunk. We will work with the telco dataset in *Chapter 6, Discovering Hunk Integration Apps*, related to custom application development. We write an Oozie coordinator, started by the Oozie server each night. Oozie is a kind of Hadoop CRON and has some additional features that help us work with data. Oozie can do many useful things, but right now we are using its basic functionality: just running the workflow each day. The coordinator code is here: `https://github.com/seregasheypak/learning-hunk/blob/master/import-milano-cdr/src/main/resources/oozie/import-milano-cdr-coord.xml`.

Next is the workflow. The coordinator is responsible for scheduling the workflow. The workflow is responsible for doing business logic. The workflow code is here: `https://github.com/seregasheypak/learning-hunk/blob/master/import-milano-cdr/src/main/resources/oozie/workflows/import-milano-cdr-wflow.xml`.

The workflow has one Sqoop action.

Next is the Sqoop action. This action declares the way the job should read data from RDBMS and store it to HDFS.

The third section is the `MapReduce` job that reads data from RDBMS and writes it to HDFS. The Sqoop action internally runs a `MapReduce` job that is responsible for getting table rows out of MySQL. The whole process sounds pretty complex, but you don't have to worry. We've created the code to implement it.

Telecommunications – SMS, Call, and Internet dataset from dandelion.eu

We are going to use several open datasets from `https://dandelion.eu`. One weekly dataset was uploaded to MySQL and contains information about the telecommunication activity in the city of Milano. Later, you will use an Oozie coordinator with the Sqoop action to create a daily partitioned dataset.

The source dataset is: `https://dandelion.eu/datagems/SpazioDati/telecom-sms-call-internet-mi/resource/` and the grid map is: `https://dandelion.eu/datagems/SpazioDati/milano-grid/resource/`.

Milano grid map

Milano is divided into equal squares. Each square has a unique ID and four longitude and latitude coordinates.

A mapping between the logical square mesh and spatial area would be helpful for us during geospatial analysis. We will demonstrate how Hunk can deal with geospatial visualizations out-of-the-box.

CDR aggregated data import process

We've prepared an Oozie coordinator to import data from MySQL to HDFS. Generally, it looks like a production-ready process. Real-life processes are organized in pretty much the same way. The following describes the idea behind the import process:

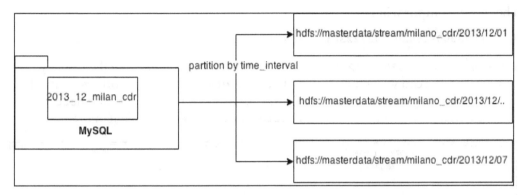

We have the potentially huge table **2013_12_milan_cdr** with time-series data. We are not going to import the whole table in one go; we will partition data using a time field named **time_interval**.

The idea is to split data by equal time periods and import it to Hadoop. It's just a projection of the RDBMS partitioning/sharing techniques to Hadoop. You'll see seven folders named from `/masterdata/stream/2013/12/01` to `07`.

You can get the workflow code here: `https://github.com/seregasheypak/` `learning-hunk/blob/master/import-milano-cdr/src/main/resources/oozie/` `workflows/import-milano-cdr-wflow.xml`.

The general idea is to:

- Run the workflow each day
- Import the data for the whole day

We've applied a dummy MySQL date function; in real life, you would use the OraOop connector, Teradata connector, or some other tricks to play with the partition properties.

Periodical data import from MySQL using Sqoop and Oozie

To run the import process, you have to open the console application inside a VM window, go to the catalog with the coordinator configuration, and submit it to Oozie:

```
cd /home/devops/oozie-configs
```
```
sudo -u hdfs oozie job -oozie http://localhost/oozie -config import-milano-cdr-coord.properties -run
```

The console output will be:

```
job: 0000000-150302102722384-oozie-oozi-C
```

Where `0000000-15030102722384-oozie-oozi-C` is the unique ID of the running coordinator. We can visit Hue and watch the progress of the import process. Visit this link: `http://localhost:8888/oozie/list_oozie_coordinators/` and `http://vm-cluster-node3.localdomain:8888/oozie/list_oozie_coordinators/`:

Here is the running coordinator. It took two minutes to import one day. There are seven days in total. We used a powerful PC (32 GB memory and an 8-core AMD CPU) to accomplish this task.

Downloading the example code

You can download the example code from `http://www.bigdatapath.com/wpcontent/uploads/2015/05/learning-hunk-05-with-mongo.zip`.

The following screenshot shows how the successful result should look:

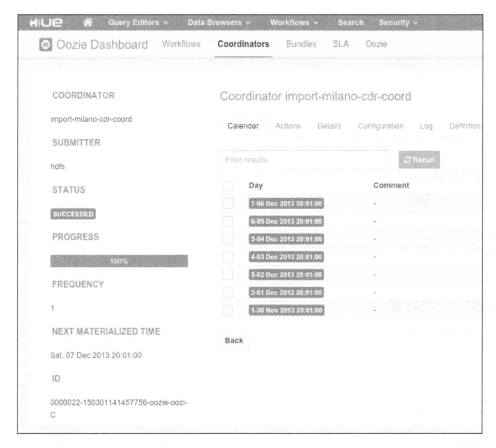

We can see that the coordinator did produce seven actions for each day starting from December 1st till December 7th.

You can use the open console application to execute this command:

```
hadoop fs -du -h /masterdata/stream/milano_cdr/2013/12
```

The output should be:

```
74.1 M    222.4 M  /masterdata/stream/milano_cdr/2013/12/01
97.0 M    291.1 M  /masterdata/stream/milano_cdr/2013/12/02
100.4 M   301.3 M  /masterdata/stream/milano_cdr/2013/12/03
100.4 M   301.1 M  /masterdata/stream/milano_cdr/2013/12/04
100.6 M   301.8 M  /masterdata/stream/milano_cdr/2013/12/05
100.6 M   301.7 M  /masterdata/stream/milano_cdr/2013/12/06
89.2 M    267.6 M  /masterdata/stream/milano_cdr/2013/12/07
```

The target format is **Avro** with snappy compression. We'll see later how Hunk works with popular storage formats and compression codecs. Avro is a reasonable choice: it has wide support across Hadoop tools and has a schema.

It's possible to skip the import process; you can move data to the target destination using a command. Open the console application and execute:

```
sudo -u hdfs hadoop fs -mkdir -p /masterdata/stream/milano_cdr/2013
sudo -u hdfs hadoop fs -mv /backup/milano_cdr/2013/12/masterdata/stream/
milano_cdr/2013/
```

Problems to solve

We have a week-length dataset with 10-minute time intervals for various subscriber activities. We are going to draw using dynamics in dimensions: part of the day, city area, and type of activity. We will build a subscriber dynamics map using imported data.

Summary

In this chapter we met big data analytics and discovered challenges that can be overcome with Hunk. In addition, we learned about Hunk's history and its internal modes. Moreover, we explored Hunk's architecture and learned about virtual indexes and ERPs. In addition, we touched on some topics related to security. Finally, we started to prepare for technical exercises by setting up Hadoop and discovering real-world use cases.

In the next chapter, we will start to explore big data in Hadoop. We will work with SPL and create amazing visualizations.

2
Explore Hadoop Data with Hunk

Hadoop has become an enterprise standard for big organizations working towards mining and implementing big data strategies. The use of Hadoop on a larger scale is set to become the new standard for practical, result-driven applications for data mining. However, it is a challenging task to extract data from Hadoop in order to explore it and find business insights. It is a fact that Hadoop provides cheap storage for any data but, unfortunately, it is inflexible for data analytics. There are plenty of tools that can add flexibility and interactivity for analytics tasks, but they have many restrictions.

Hunk avoids the main drawbacks of big data analytics and offers rich functionality and interactivity for analytics.

In this chapter you will learn how to deploy Hunk on top of Hadoop in order to start discovering Hunk. In addition, we will load data into Hadoop and will discover it via Hunk, using the **Splunk Processing Language** (**SPL**). Finally, we will learn about Hunk security.

Setting up Hunk

In order to start exploring Hadoop data, we have to install Hunk on top of our Hadoop Cluster. Hunk is easy to install and configure. Let's learn how to deploy Hunk version 6.2.1 on top of an existing CDH cluster. It's assumed that your VM is up and running.

Extracting Hunk to a VM

1. Open the console application.

2. Run `ls -la` to see the list of files in your home directory:

   ```
   [cloudera@quickstart ~]$ cd ~

   [cloudera@quickstart ~]$ ls -la | grep hunk

   -rw-r--r--   1 root       root      113913609 Mar 23 04:09 hunk-
   6.2.1-249325-Linux-x86_64.tgz
   ```

3. Unpack the archive:

   ```
   cd /opt
   sudo tar xvzf /home/cloudera/hunk-6.2.1-249325-Linux-x86_64.tgz -C
   /opt
   ```

Setting up Hunk variables and configuration files

1. It's time to set the `SPLUNK_HOME` environment variable. This variable has already been added to the profile:

   ```
   export SPLUNK_HOME=/opt/hunk
   ```

2. Use the default `splunk-launch.conf`. This is the basic properties file used by the Hunk service. We don't have to change anything special, so let's use the default settings:

   ```
   Sudo cp /opt/hunk/etc/splunk-launch.conf.default /opt/hunk//etc/
   splunk-launch.conf
   ```

Running Hunk for the first time

Run Hunk using the following command:

```
sudo /opt/hunk/bin/splunk start --accept-license
```

Here is the sample output from the first run:

```
This appears to be your first time running this version of Splunk.

Copying '/opt/hunk/etc/openldap/ldap.conf.default' to '/opt/hunk/etc/
openldap/ldap.conf'.

Generating RSA private key, 1024 bit long modulus


Some output lines were deleted to reduce amount of log text
```

```
Waiting for web server at http://127.0.0.1:8000 to be available.... Done
```

```
If you get stuck, we're here to help.
Look for answers here: http://docs.splunk.com
```

```
The Splunk web interface is at http://vm-cluster-node1.localdomain:8000
```

Now you can access the Hunk UI using `http://localhost:8000` in the browser on your virtual machine.

Setting up a data provider and virtual index for CDR data

We need to accomplish two tasks: providing a technical connector to underlying data storage and creating a virtual index for data on this storage.

Log in to `http://localhost:8000`. The system will ask you to change the default admin user password. I have set it to `admin`.

Setting up a connection to Hadoop

Right now we are ready to set up integration between Hadoop and Hunk. First we need to specify the way Hunk connects to the current Hadoop installation. We are using the most recent way: YARN with MR2. Then we have to point the virtual indexes to data stored in Hadoop:

1. Click on **Explore Data**.

2. Click on **Create a provider** on the next screen:

Let's fill in the form to create a data provider. The data provider component is used to interact with frameworks such as Hadoop. You should set up the necessary properties in order to make sure the provider correctly gets data from the underlying datasource. We will also create a data provider for Mongo later in this book. You don't have to install something special. Cloudera VM, used as a base for this example, carries all the necessary software. Java JDK 1.7 is on board already.

Property name	Value
Name	hadoop-hunk-provider
Java home	/usr/java/jdk1.7.0_67-cloudera
Hadoop home	/usr/lib/hadoop
Hadoop version	Hadoop 2.x, (Yarn)
Filesystem	hdfs://quickstart.cloudera:8020
Resource Manager Address	quickstart.cloudera:8032
Resource Scheduler Address	quickstart.cloudera:8030
HDFS Working Directory	/user/hunk
Job Queue	default

You don't have to modify any other properties. The HDFS working directory has been created for you in advance. You can create it using this command:

```
sudo -u hdfshadoop fs  -mkdir -p /user/hunk
```

You should see the following screen, if you did everything correctly:

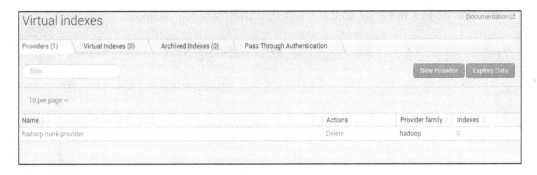

Let's discuss briefly what we have done:

- We told Hunk where Hadoop home and Java are. Hunk uses Hadoop streaming internally so it needs to know how to call Java and Hadoop streaming. You can inspect submitted jobs from Hunk (discussed later) and view these lines:

```
/opt/hunk/bin/jars/sudobash /usr/bin/hadoop jar "/opt/hunk/bin/
jars/SplunkMR-s6.0-hy2.0.jar" "com.splunk.mr.SplunkMR"
```

- A MapReduce JAR is submitted by Hunk. Also we need to tell Hunk where the YARN resource manager and scheduler are located. These services allow us to ask for cluster resources and run jobs.

- Job queues could be useful in a production environment. You could have several queues for cluster resource distribution in real life. We will set the queue name as `default` since we are not discussing cluster utilization and load balancing.

Setting up a virtual index for data stored in Hadoop

Now it's time to create a virtual index. We are going to add a dataset with AVRO files to the virtual index as example data. We will work with that index later in *Chapter 6, Discovering Hunk Integration Apps*.

1. Click on **Explore Data** and then click on **Create a virtual index** on the next screen:

2. You'll get a message to the effect that there are **No indexes**:

3. Just click on **New Virtual Index.**

   A virtual index is metadata; it tells Hunk where data is located and what provider should be used to read that data. The virtual index goal is to declare access to data. That data could be structured or unstructured. A virtual index is immutable; you can only read data through that type of index. The data provider tells Hunk how to read data and the virtual index declares the data properties.

Property name	Value
Name	`milano_cdr_aggregated_10_min_activity`
Path to data in HDFS	`/masterdata/stream/milano_cdr`

4. Here is an example of the screen you should see after creating the first virtual index.

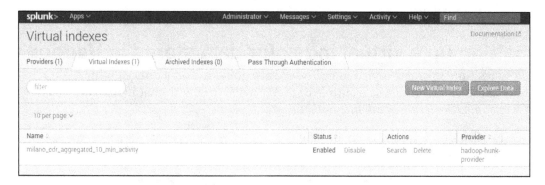

Accessing data through a virtual index

1. Click on **Explore Data** and **Select a Provider and Virtual Index**:

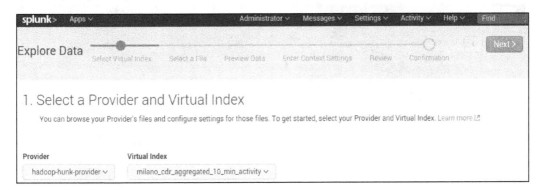

2. Select part-m-00000.avro by clicking on it. The **Next** Button will be activated after you pick a file:

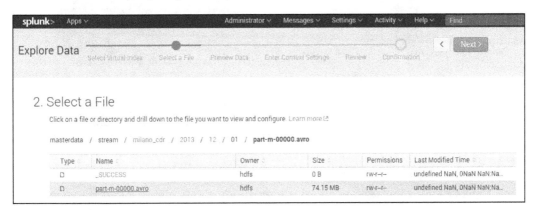

3. Preview the data on the **Preview data** step in the wizard. You should see how Hunk automatically formats the timestamp from our CDR data.

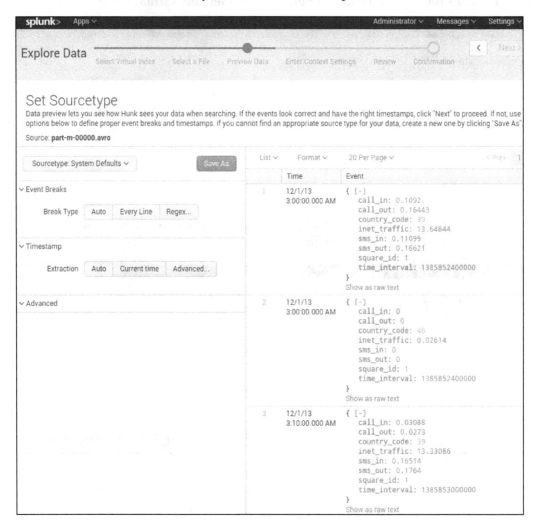

Pay attention to the **Time** column and the field named `time_interval` in the **Event** column. The `time_interval` field keeps the time of the record. Hunk should automatically use that field as the time field, which allows you to run a search query using a time range. It's a typical pattern for reading time series data.

4. Save the source type by clicking on **Save as** then click on **Next**.

5. At the step **Enter Context Settings** choose **Application Context**, than in **Sharing context** choose **All apps**, then click on **Next**.

6.   The last step allows you to review what you've done:

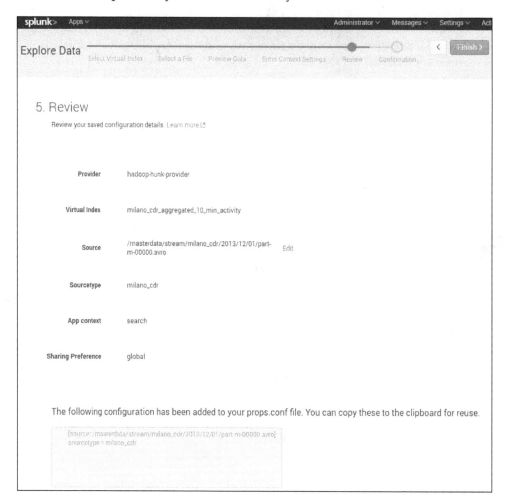

7.   Click on **Finish** to create final wizard.

Exploring data

We are going to explore Apache web logs taken from the online store. These logs are taken from the Apache web server and uploaded to HDFS. You'll see how to read Apache logs out of the box. The name of the store is unicorn fashion. Here is an example log line:

```
135.51.156.129 - - [02/Dec/2013:13:52:29] "POST /product.screen?productNa
me=SHORTS&JSESSIONID=CA10MO9AZ5USANA4955 HTTP 1.1" 200 2334 "http://www.
yahoo.com" "Opera/9.01 (Windows NT 5.1; U; en)" 167
```

It's a normal Apache access combined log. We can build reports, dashboards, and alerts on top of this data. You will:

- Learn the basics of SPL to create queries
- Learn visualization abilities
- Drill-down from the aggregated report to the underlying detailed data
- Check the job details used to prepare report data
- Create alerts and see a simple alert use-case
- Create a dashboard presenting web analytics reports on a single page
- Create a virtual index

You know already how to create a virtual index; we provide a screenshot with an index configuration:

Name *

digital_analytics

Description

Provider

hadoop-hunk-provider ∨

Paths

Path to data in HDFS ? *

/staging/web_logs

Example: /home/data/apache/logs/

Creating reports

Let's try to create some reports in order to meet basic functionality of Hunk and Search Processing Language (SPL).

The top five browsers report

Let's get the top five browsers used by online store visitors. We need to start the **Explore data** wizard:

1. Go to **Virtual indexes**:

2. Click on **Explore Data**.

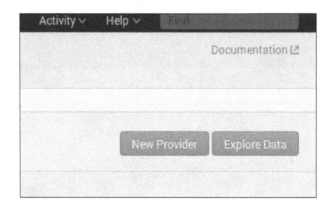

3. Pick the Hadoop provider and our `digital_analytics` virtual index:

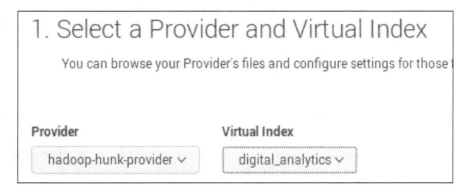

4. Select a file and click on **Next**:

5. Select **Web | Access combined** as a type for logs:

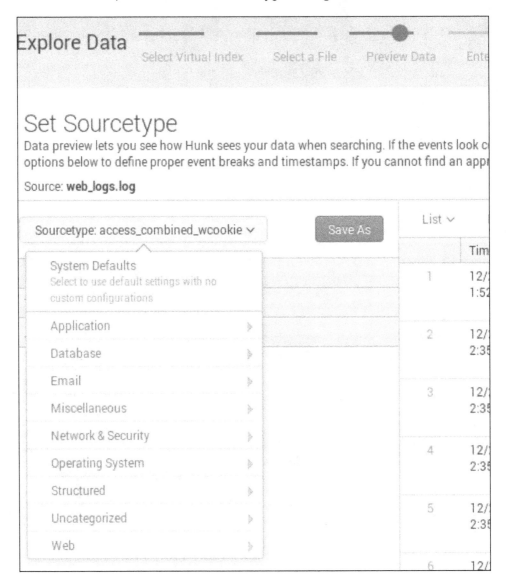

Your screen should look like this:

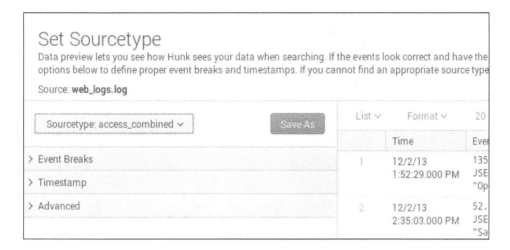

6. Complete the context settings:

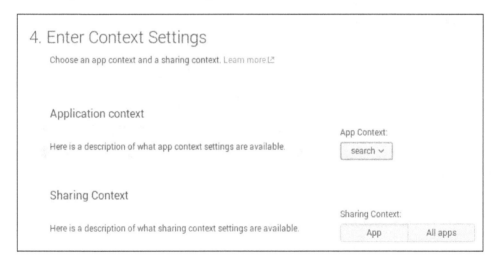

7. Choose **search** in **App Context** and select **App** under **Sharing Context**.

8. Review the settings and click on **Finish**. Now we are ready to create our first dashboard.

9. Open `http://quickstart.cloudera:8000/en-US/app/launcher/home` and click on **Search & Reporting**:

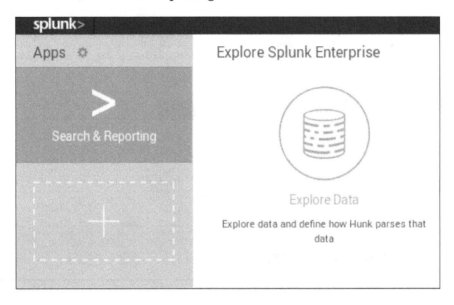

10. Use a query to get the top five browsers:

    ```
    index="digital_analytics" | top 5 useragent
    ```

    The search interface in front of you should look like this:

11. Save the report by selecting **Save As | Report** from the drop-down list:

12. The settings for the report to be saved are as follows:

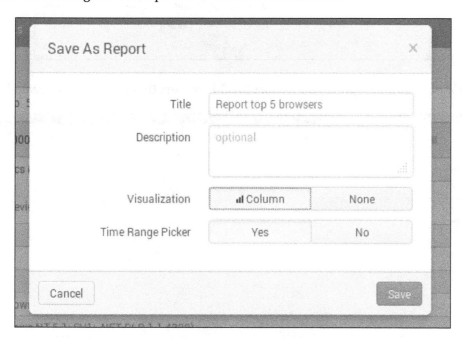

13. The report will have visualizations in the **Column** and **Time Range Picker** controls.

14. Here is the final result. Go to the **Reports** page:

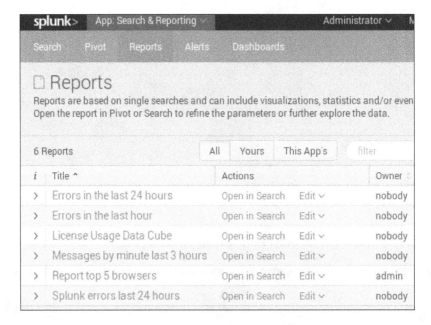

15. Select the report named **Report top 5 browsers** that we have just created:

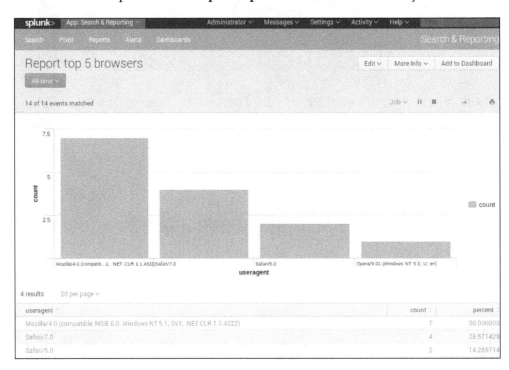

Top referrers

Let's create one more report. We are going to display the sources of site traffic. Go back to the query search and use the following expression to get referrers:

```
index="digital_analytics" referer != *unicorn*| top referer
percentfield=percent
```

You should read the expression in this way:

1. Use the `digital_analytics` index.

2. Exclude lines where the referrer field contains the `unicorn` substring.

3. Group by the referrer field value, count those lines having the same referrer value, and order counts in descending order.

> You can read more about `top` command here: `http://docs.splunk.com/Documentation/Splunk/6.2.2/SearchReference/Top`.

4. Check your search result page:

5. Check the job statistics.

> Hunk provides you with a nice way to get access to job counters and logs. This could be useful later when you are interested in fine-tuning performance.

6. Click on **Job** and select **Inspect Job** from the drop-down list:

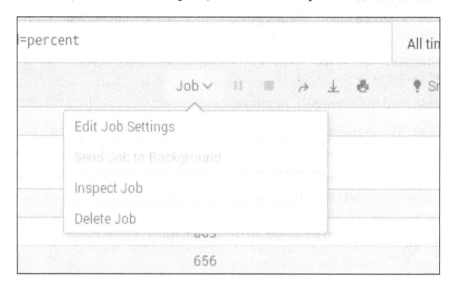

You'll see a nice job report providing insights into why it's so slow or extremely fast. There is also a link to a log file. You might need it later if you encounter errors:

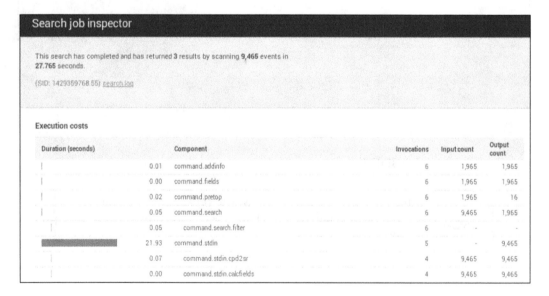

Search job inspector

This search has completed and has returned 3 results by scanning 9,465 events in 27.765 seconds.

(SID: 1429359768.55) search.log

Execution costs

Duration (seconds)		Component	Invocations	Input count	Output count
	0.01	command.addinfo	6	1,965	1,965
	0.00	command.fields	6	1,965	1,965
	0.02	command.pretop	6	1,965	16
	0.05	command.search	6	9,465	1,965
	0.05	command.search.filter	6	.	.
	21.93	command.stdin	5	.	9,465
	0.07	command.stdin.cpd2sr	4	9,465	9,465
	0.00	command.stdin.calcfields	4	9,465	9,465

7. Select a visualization for the report. Click on the **Visualization** tab and select a pie chart from the **Drilldown** option:

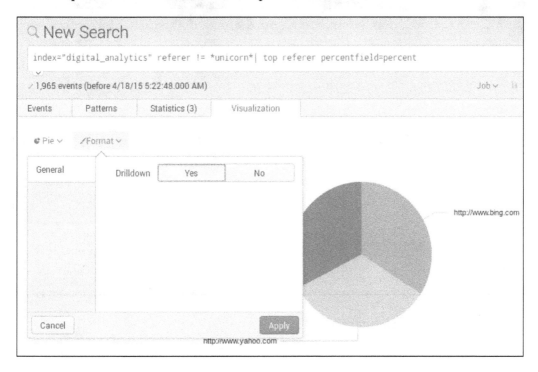

8. You can click on the pie and get detailed information. Click on any sector:

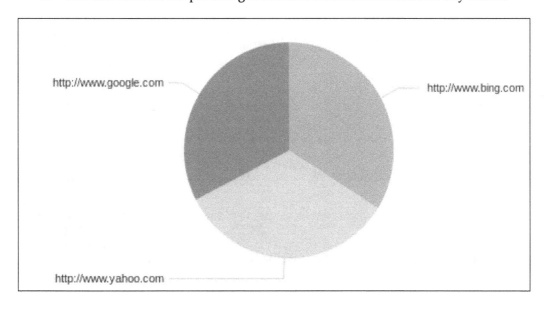

9. Hunk will automatically create a query for you to display detailed data:

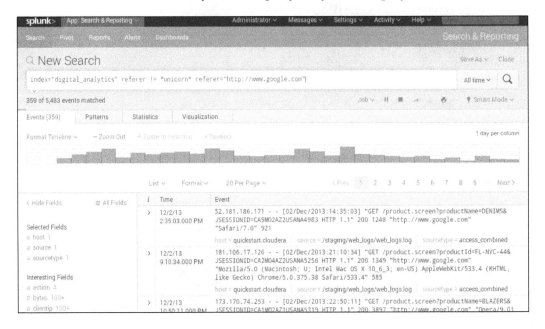

10. Save the top referrer report:

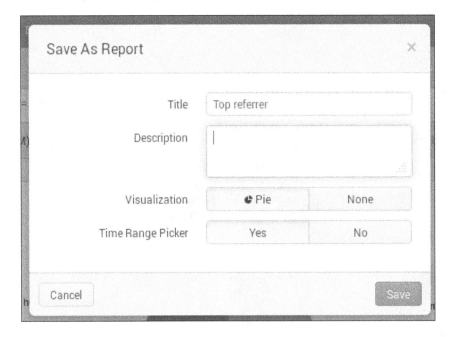

Site errors report

Let's perform naive analytics to count the errors occurring on our site.

1. See the statuses logged by the Apache server.

    ```
    index="digital_analytics" | chart count by status
    ```

    Use bars to visualize the result:

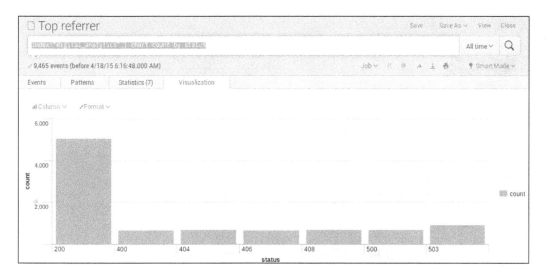

We see various status codes. Let's pay special attention to code=500, which indicates an error on the server side.

2. Calculate the error ratio using the `eval` expression.

    ```
    index="digital_analytics" | eval errorRatio = if (status ==500,
    "ERROR", "ELSE") | timechart count by errorRatio | sort -
    errorRatio
    ```

    The idea of the expression is to:

    1. Use the `digital_analytics` index.
    2. Calculate the field with the name `errorRatio`. If the `status` field in the index has the value `500`, then `errorRatio` = «ERROR»; otherwise, the `errorRatio` field gets the value «ELSE».

3. Count `errorRatio` occurrences over time and sort by the count of `errorRatio`:

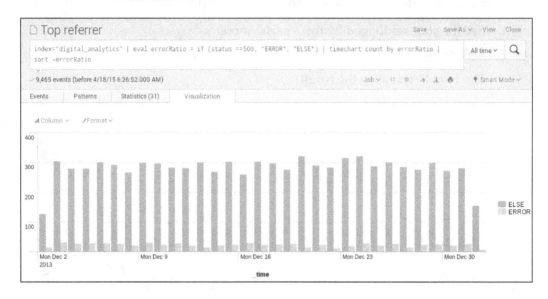

3. Save the report:

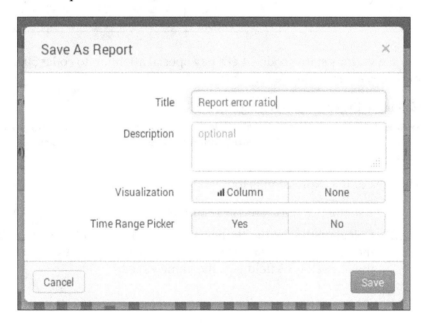

Creating alerts

Hunk can issue alerts when a condition is met. Let's configure an alert when the error count threshold is reached.

1. Use a query to count the status with code =500, which signifies an error on the server side:

   ```
   index="digital_analytics" status=500 | stats count
   ```

2. This query returns the error count. Select **Save As | Alert**:

It's hard to emulate scheduled activity right now; let's pick the most simple case and see how it works generally.

> You should definitely choose the scheduled type of alert in production. The idea is to run the query periodically and issue an alert. It could optionally be sent as an email so the operator can react appropriately.

The following screenshot shows the settings for saving a new alert:

3. We've chosen **Per-Result** to get an alert each time the report returns something.

4. Set the alert to be displayed by selecting **Activity | Triggered Alerts**:

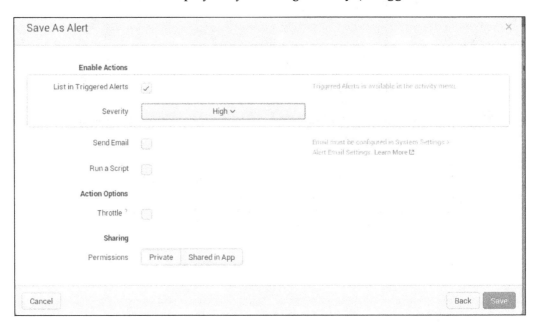

The following screenshot is an overview of the created alert:

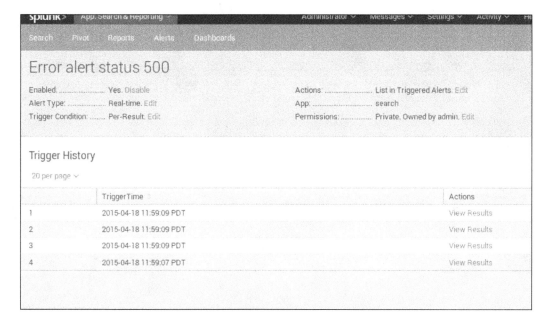

5. Go to **Activity** | **Triggered Alerts** and confirm that the alert has been published:

Creating a dashboard

Now it's time to see how dashboards work. Let's find regions where visitors get problems (status = 500) while using our online store:

```
index="digital_analytics" status=500 | iplocation clientip | geostats
latfield=lat longfield=lon count by Country
```

You should see a map showing country errors:

Now let's save this as a dashboard. Click on **Save As** and select **Dashboard Panel** from the drop-down menu:

The following screenshot shows the values for fields in the **Save** form:

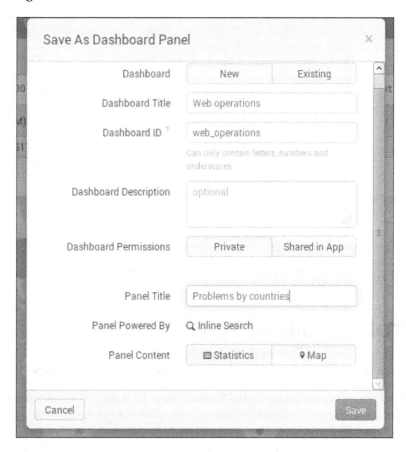

You should get a new dashboard with a single panel and our report on it. We have several previously created reports. Let's add them to the newly created dashboard using separate panels. Click on **Edit | Edit Panels**:

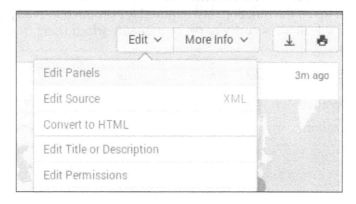

Select **Add new panel** | **New from report** and add one of our reports:

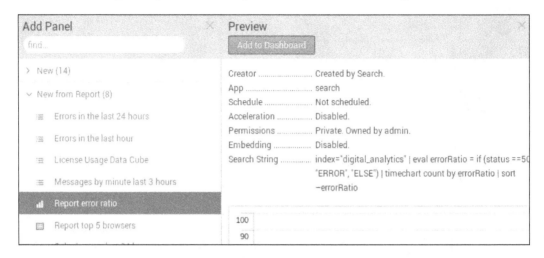

You should get one page with four reports at the end.

Controlling security with Hunk

What is security? We could work on data security forever; this part of IT infrastructure is infinite. Companies are usually interested in these aspects:

- **User/group/access control list-based access to data**: Administrators should have something similar to the read/write/execute in Linux. We can set who owns the data and who can read/write it.

- **Audit/log access to data**: We need to know who got access to data, and when and how.

- **Isolation**: We don't want our data to be publicly accessible. We would like to set access to clusters from specific subnets, for example. We are not going to try to set up all the functionality required for production-ready security. Our aim is to set simple security to prevent unauthorized users from accessing the data.

What is data security? It consists of three major parts:

- Authentication
- Authorization
- Audit

These three properties give us a clue as to who did something somewhere, and which privileges were used. Hadoop security setup is still a non-trivial task. Let's try to implement basic authentication and authorization.

There are several approaches to securing your clusters. We recommend isolating clusters using VPN since it's one of the easiest ways to protect data and get basic authentication with audit logging. You can always do non-trivial installations, and the best approach is to clearly estimate how much time you will spend setting up Kerberos. Usually, you don't have time for that; it's all devoted to reaching business goals. See the examples on the Internet where a younger startup's security fails and exposes private data to hackers. You definitely need to read a dedicated book devoted to Hadoop security with Kerberos enabled if you need really strong security.

> There is a joke about Kerberos and Hadoop. You can join Hadoop user groups or just search them via the keywords *Kerberos, Enable, Help, stopped working*. Sometimes, a guy asks a group, "How can I set up Kerberos for my cluster?" He gets some general considerations and links to documents. Then in few days the guy appears again in a group with this question: "How can I disable Kerberos on my Hadoop; everything has stopped working?".

We are going to touch on the following topics briefly:

- What is the *default* Hadoop security?
- How Hunk runs out of the box on top of Hadoop
- What is pass-through authentication?
- How to configure pass-through authentication for Hunk and Hadoop using Hunk UI:
    - One Hunk user to one Hadoop user
    - Many Hunk users to one Hadoop user
    - Hunk user(s) to the same Hadoop user with different queues
- How Kerberos works for Hadoop and Hunk

The default Hadoop security

The default Hadoop security is designed to stop good people doing the wrong things, so security is the wrong term for the default functionality. HDFS acts as the base system for storing data with redundancy and even distribution features, which leads to an even cluster load and resilience to node failures. Consider that HDFS is a traditional file system that spans across many nodes. You can configure HDFS not to have SPOF (see the NameNode HA configuration). Be aware, that you can totally lose some of your nodes with data without noticing it if you don't have any monitoring and alerting. (if you don't have monitoring and alerting of course). Let's see what Hadoop HDFS suggests you do out of the box. We need to open the terminal on our VM:

1. List the HDFS directories:

    Type:

    ```
    hadoop fs -ls /
    ```

    And get output:

    ```
    [cloudera@quickstart ~]$ hadoop fs -ls /
    Found 9 items
    drwxr-xr-x   - cloudera supergroup          0 2015-03-16 06:27 /
    applications
    drwxr-xr-x   - hdfs     supergroup          0 2015-03-16 07:26 /
    backup
    some output removed to reduce size of logs.
    drwxr-xr-x   - hdfs     supergroup          0 2014-12-18 04:32 /
    var
    ```

    You see the listing for the root of HDFS. HDFS is not fully POSIX-compliant, but you can see traditional user and group ownerships for catalogs with masks. x is used only for listing the catalog. There are no executables on HDFS.

2. Check your current OS user. This user on OS and Hadoop tools will use this username while interacting with the HDFS file system:

    ```
    [cloudera@quickstart ~]$ whoami
    cloudera
    ```

    Your current user should be cloudera.

3. Check the group membership for your OS user:

    ```
    [cloudera@quickstart ~]$ groups
    cloudera default
    ```

    Your cloudera user is a member of two groups: cloudera and default.

4. Create a file on HDFS.

   This command creates an empty file in your current HDFS home directory. Yes, HDFS also has home directories for users:

   ```
   [cloudera@quickstart ~]$ hadoop fs -touchz file_on_hdfs
   ```

5. Now verify that the file was created and exists in your home directory.

6. The `hadoop fs` command points to your HDFS home directory by default:

   ```
   [cloudera@quickstart ~]$ hadoop fs -ls
   Found 2 items
   drwxr-xr-x   - cloudera cloudera          0 2015-03-16 06:41
   .Trash
   -rw-r--r--   1 cloudera cloudera          0 2015-04-05 10:14 file_
   on_hdfs
   ```

7. You can type the absolute path to your HDFS home directory; the result will be the same:

   ```
   [cloudera@quickstart ~]$ hadoop fs -ls /user/cloudera
   Found 2 items
   drwxr-xr-x   - cloudera cloudera          0 2015-03-16 06:41 /
   user/cloudera/.Trash
   -rw-r--r--   1 cloudera cloudera          0 2015-04-05 10:14 /
   user/cloudera/file_on_hdfs
   ```

   The `file_on_hdfs` file has been created and its size is 0 bytes. The file belongs to the `cloudera` user because you are logged in as `cloudera`. Members of the group named `cloudera` (rw-r--r--) can read this file. Others also can read (-rw-r--r--). Only the `cloudera` user can modify the file (-rw-r--r--).

8. Try to modify file using another user:

   1. Create a file:

      ```
      echo  "new line for file" > append.txt
      ```

   2. Try to append this to the existing file using a user who is not allowed to modify the file:

      ```
      sudo su hdfs hadoop fs -appendToFile append.txt /user/
      cloudera/file_on_hdfs
      ```

3. No problem; you can append to the file. It's counterintuitive since access flags tell us that the HDFS user can't modify the file owned by the `cloudera` user. Let's double-check that we did the append operation:

```
[cloudera@quickstart ~]$ hadoop fs -cat /user/cloudera/file_
on_hdfs

new line for file
```

9. Fix the `namenode` configuration.

The explanation is easy: `namenode` is a service responsible for HFDS metadata, such as access permissions. Right now it's up and running, but doesn't take care of owners for files and catalogs. Let's fix it. There are two properties responsible for the behavior we need:

  ◦ `dfs.permissions`
  ◦ `dfs.permissions.enabled`

The first one is old and will be deprecated in the near future; the second one is new. Let's turn both to `true`.

10. Go to `/etc/Hadoop/conf/hdfs-site.xml`. Find and change both properties to `true`. You can use a visual editor and file browser if you are not familiar with the console `vi` tool:

```
<property>
      <name>dfs.permissions.enabled</name>
      <value>true</value>
  </property>
  <property>
      <name>dfs.permissions</name>
      <value>true</value>
  </property>
  <property>
      <name>hadoop.proxyuser.root.hosts</name>
      <value>*</value>
  </property>
  <property>
      <name>hadoop.proxyuser.root.groups</name>
      <value>*</value>
  </property>
```

11. Restart NameNode to make it see the new configuration:

```
[cloudera@quickstart ~]$ sudo /etc/init.d/hadoop-hdfs-namenode
stop

stopping namenode
```

```
Stopped Hadoop namenode:                                    [  OK
]

[cloudera@quickstart ~]$ sudo /etc/init.d/hadoop-hdfs-namenode
start

starting namenode, logging to /var/log/hadoop-hdfs/hadoop-hdfs-
namenode-quickstart.cloudera.out

Started Hadoop namenode:                                    [  OK
]
```

12. Try to modify the HDFS file using the `mail` user, who definitely doesn't have any rights to modify the file:

```
[cloudera@quickstart ~]$ sudo -u mail hadoop fs -appendToFile
append.txt /user/cloudera/file_on_hdfs

appendToFile: Permission denied: user=mail, access=WRITE, inode="/
user/cloudera/file_on_hdfs":cloudera:cloudera:-rw-r--r--
```

Great, we see that owner permissions are preserved and you are not allowed to modify the file using the `mail` user since only the `cloudera` user has write access to it.

One Hunk user to one Hadoop user

We've installed Hunk with a default user, named admin. Security was totally disabled while we were adding the first virtual index on top of the aggregated Milano city telco data. Now we've enabled permission checks and the admin user cannot have access to data stored in HDFS. We are going to map the Hunk user named `admin` to the user named `mail` and see that it's impossible to access data in HDFS through the `mail` user since this user doesn't have proper access to data.

1. Open the console to create a file in HDFS with data and change permissions:

```
#create catalog on HDFS
hadoop fs -mkdir -p /staging/test_access_using_mail


#create file locally
echo  "new line for file" > file_with_data.txt


#copy locally created file to HDFS
hadoop fs -copyFromLocal file_with_data.txt /staging/test_access_
using_mail


#change permissions to restrict access from any except owner
hadoop fs -chmod -R 700 /staging/test_access_using_mail
```

2. Enable pass-through authentication for the provider.

    We created a provider previously. Now it's time to enable pass-through authentication there. Hunk will use the user to impersonalize itself while interacting with HDFS. The idea is simple:

    ◦   Enable pass-through authentication.

    ◦   Set mapping between the Hunk user and the user from HDFS. We impersonalize the default Hunk `admin` user and impersonalize the `mail` user to interact with HDFS.

    ◦   Open the **Virtual indexes** menu located under the **DATA** header:

3. Select the previously created provider for Hadoop:

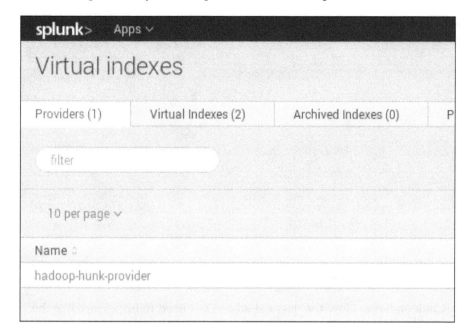

4. Enable pass-through authentication. Scroll down and click on **Save**:

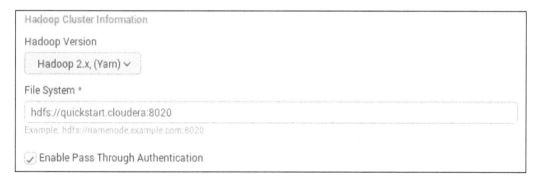

5. Set up mapping between the Hunk `admin` user and the user named `mail`:

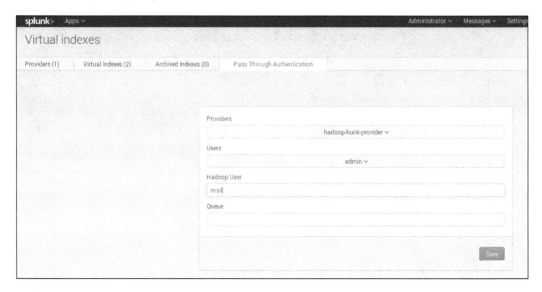

6. Click on **Save**. Now the user called `mail` is used to impersonalize the `admin` user.

7. Create a new virtual index and verify that the `mail` user can't access data because it lacks the necessary permissions.

   The following screenshot shows the settings for the new virtual index that we can't access via the `mail` user:

8. Explore data using the Hadoop provider and the new index.

9. Select the provider with enabled pass-through authentication and the newly created index:

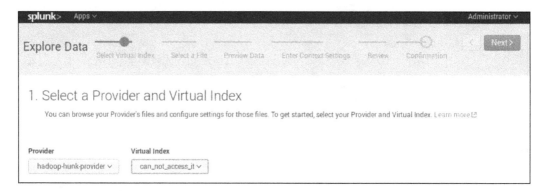

10. You should see a blank screen:

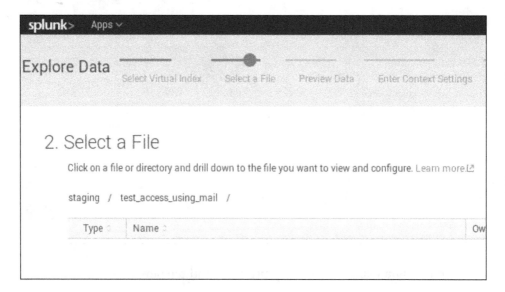

11. Use the `cloudera` user for impersonalization and to get access to data.

12. We've created a file from the user named `cloudera` and set access rights to `700`, which means only the `cloudera` user can access the file. Open the **Pass Through Authentication** form and replace `mail` with `cloudera`:

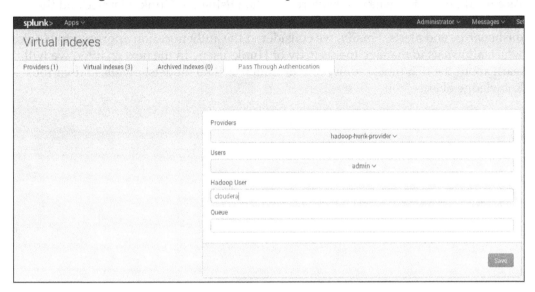

13. Repeat the **Explore Data** wizard process; now you should see the file:

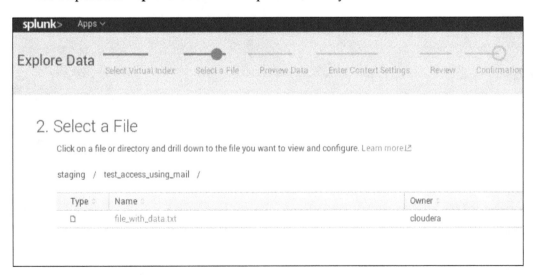

Summary

In this chapter, we have created a Hadoop connector and virtual index for CDR data. As a result, we got a chance to explore that data using the Hunk interface and the Splunk Search Processing Language. In addition, we learnt how to create reports, dashboards, and alerts. Finally, we considered the authentication approach to Hunk, which allows us to manage the security of Hunk, users. In the next chapter, we will learn about the rich functionality of Hunk such as data models, pivots, and various knowledge objects.

3

Meeting Hunk Features

Big data analytics is a very popular trend. As a result, most business users want to discover their big data using intuitive and user-friendly tools because exploring data stored in Hadoop or any NoSQL data stores is a challenging task. Fortunately, Hunk does away with all the complexity obstructing analysts and business users. Moreover, it gives additional features that allow us to handle big data in just several mouse clicks. This is possible with Hunk knowledge objects.

In the previous chapter, we created virtual indexes based on web logs for the international fashion retailer Unicorn Fashion. We created some queries and reports via **Search Processing Language** (**SPL**). Moreover, we created a web operation dashboard and learnt how to create alerts.

In this chapter, we will explore Hunk knowledge objects, which will help us to achieve better results with less effort. Moreover, we will become familiar with pivots and data models, in order to learn how to work with Hunk with the traditional **Business Intelligence** (**BI**) tool.

Knowledge objects

Hunk has the same capabilities as Splunk; as a result we can create various knowledge objects that can help us explore big data and make it more user-friendly.

 A knowledge object is a configuration within Hunk that uses permissions and is controlled via the Hunk access control layer. Knowledge objects can be scoped to specific applications. Read/write permissions for them are granted to roles.

To work with knowledge objects, go to the **KNOWLEDGE** menu under **Settings**:

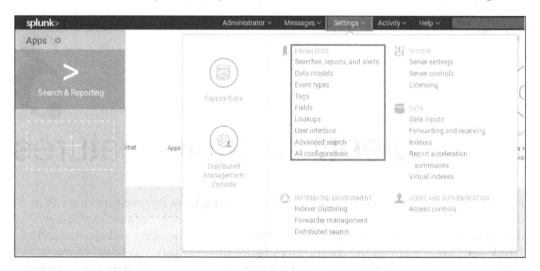

There are various knowledge objects available in Hunk. We encountered SPL, reports, dashboards, and alerts in the previous chapter. Let's expand our knowledge of Hunk and explore additional knowledge objects.

For more information about knowledge objects, see:
`http://docs.splunk.com/Documentation/Splunk/`
`latest/Knowledge/WhatisSplunkknowledge.`

Field aliases

Field aliases help us to normalize data over several sources. We can create multiple aliases in one field.

Aliases should be applied after field extraction, before lookups. In addition, we can apply field aliases to lookups.

Let's create a new alias using the following steps:

1. Go to **Settings** | **Fields** | **Field aliases**.
2. Click on **Add new**.

3. Enter the **Name** as Web Browser, type the **sourcetype** as access_combined, create this alias under **Field aliases**: useragent = web_browser, and click **Save** — as shown in the following screenshot:

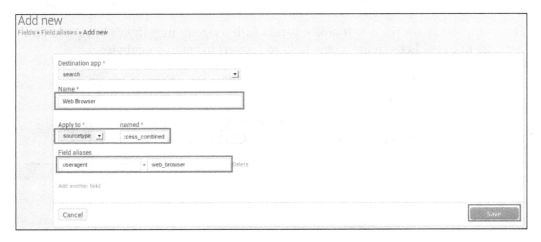

4. Change sharing permissions to **This app only (search)**.
5. Go to search and run: index="digital_analytics".
6. Then look at the fields. There is a new field — web_browser:

Moreover, we can create the same alias web_browser for any other data source. For example, we could have other logs, where instead of useragent we could just have agent. In this case, we can create a new alias that will map agent as web_browser. As a result, we create one alias for two different fields from various data sources.

Calculated fields

A calculated field acts as a shortcut for performing repetitive, long, or complex transformations using the eval command.

Calculated fields must be based upon an extracted or discovered field. It is impossible to create a calculated field based on another calculated field.

For example, say we want to monitor bandwidth usage in megabytes but we have all our data in bytes. Let's create a new field to convert bytes to megabytes:

1. Go to **Settings** | **Fields** | **Calculated fields**.

2. Click on **Add new**.

3. Type the **sourcetype** as `access_combined`, the **Name** as `bandwidth`, and **Eval expression** as `bytes/1024/1024`. Click on **Save**:

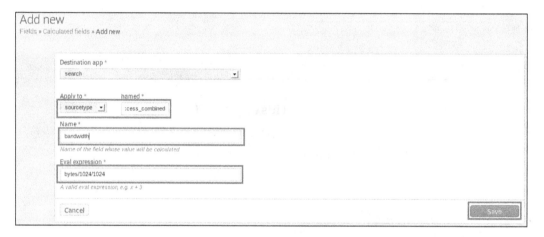

4. Change the sharing permissions for the new field to **This app only (search)**.

5. Go to search and run the new query in order to measure the bandwidth across countries and find the most popular countries:

```
index="digital_analytics" | iplocation clientip |stats
sum(bandwidth) by Country | sort - sum(bandwidth)
```

As a result, we got the top countries and their bandwidth in megabytes and used the new calculated field in a search like any other extracted field.

Field extractions

Field extractions are a special utility that helps us create custom fields. It generates a regular expression that pulls those fields from similar events. We can extract fields that are static and often needed in searches using **Interactive Field Extractor (IFX)**. It is a very useful tool that:

- Has graphical UI
- Generates regex for us
- Ensures extracted fields persist as a knowledge object
- Is reusable in multiple searches

Let's try to extract new fields from our digital data set:

1. Run a search using the following query:

   ```
   index="digital_analytics"
   ```

2. Select **Extract Fields** from the **Event** actions menu as shown in the following screenshot:

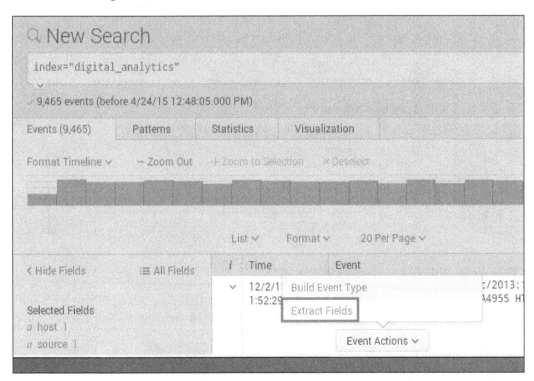

3. The new window will appear; we can highlight one or more values in the sample event to create fields. In our case, we want to extract just the name of the browser without the version or any other information. We should highlight the name of browser, give the name, and click on **Add Extraction**:

4. The next step is validation. We can take a quick look at how Hunk extracted the browser name from other events:

5. Click **Next**, change the app permission as usual for the app, and click on **Finish**.

6. We can check the result; just run a new query in the search app:

```
index="digital_analytics" | stats count by browser_name
```

Moreover, there is another way to extract fields during the search using the rex and erex commands.

 You can learn more about the rex and erex commands, with examples, at: http://docs.splunk.com/Documentation/Splunk/6.2.2/SearchReference/Erex and http://docs.splunk.com/Documentation/Splunk/latest/SearchReference/Rex.

Tags

Tags are like nicknames that you create for related field/value pairs. They can make our data more understandable and less ambiguous. It is possible to create several tags for any field/value combination.

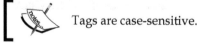 Tags are case-sensitive.

Let's create tags for our data set:

1. Run a search with the following query:

   ```
   index="digital_analytics"
   ```

2. Click on the arrow for event details. Then, under **action** click on the down arrow and select **Edit Tags** for the **action** field:

3. Name the tag **Checkout** and click on **Save**.

4. Let's check our new tag. Run a new query:

   ```
   index="digital_analytics" tag="Checkout"
   ```

We get the following result with our new tag:

Event type

An event type is a method of categorizing events based on a search; in other words, we can create a group of events based on common values. Let's look at the following example in order to better understand how this works. We can create a new event to:

- Categorize specific key/value pairs
- Classify search strings

- Tag event types to organize data in categories
- Identify fields we can report on

For example, say the sales team wants to track monthly online sales. They want to easily identify purchases that are categorized by item. Let's create a new event type for coats:

1. Run a search using the following query:

   `index="digital_analytics" action=purchase productName=COATS`

2. Click on **Save As | Event Type**:

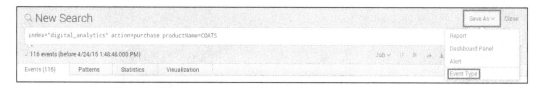

3. Type the name as `Purchase Coats`. In addition, we can create a new tag and choose the color and priority. Then click on **Save**.

4. Go to **Settings | Event Type** and change permissions for our event type as usual.

5. We can check this by running a new query:

   `index="digital_analytics" action=purchase.`

6. There will be a new and interesting field: `eventtype`. As a result, we can group our events in custom groups using tags and event types.

Workflow actions

Workflow actions launch from fields and events in our search results in order to interact with external resources or narrow our search. The possible actions are:

- **GET**: This is used to pass information to an external web resource
- **POST**: This is used to send field values to an external resource
- **Search**: This uses field values to perform a secondary search

For example, organizations often need to track ongoing attempts by external sources trying to log in with invalid credentials. We can use a GET workflow action that will open a new browser window with information about the source IP address.

For more information about workflow actions in the Splunk knowledgebase with detailed explanations and examples, see: `http://docs.splunk.com/Documentation/Splunk/latest/Knowledge/CreateworkflowactionsinSplunkWeb`.

Macros

Macros are useful when we frequently run searches with a similar search syntax. It can be a full search string or a portion of a search that can be reused in multiple places. In addition, macros allow us to define one or more arguments within the search segment.

Let's create macros with an argument:

1. Go to **Settings | Advanced search | Search macros**.

2. Click **Add new** and type the name as `activitybycategory(2)`.

3. Enter the search string:

    ```
    index="digital_analytics" action=$action1$   AND
    productName=$Name1$  |  stats count by product_name
    ```

4. In the **Arguments** field type these arguments: `action1`, `Name1`. We should get the following:

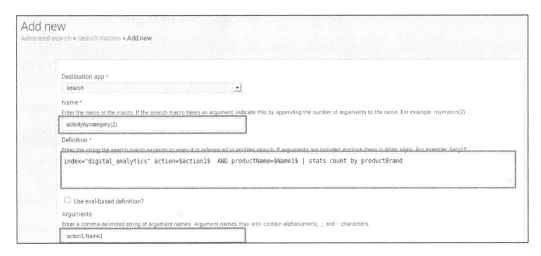

5. Let's try to run our macros. Type in a search and run it:

    ```
    activitybycategory(purchase,COATS)
    ```

6. As a result, we get a result that is similar to running an ordinary search:

```
index="digital_analytics" action=purchase  AND productName=COATS |
stats count by productName
```

Data model

A data model is a hierarchically structured data set that generates searches and drives a **pivot**. (A pivot is an interface in which we can create reports based on data models. Soon we will explore pivots more closely.) In other words, data models provide a more meaningful representation of underlying raw machine data.

Data models are designed to make it easy to share and reuse domain knowledge. The idea is that admins or powerusers create data models for non-technical users, who interact with data via a user-friendly pivot UI.

Let's create a data model for our digital data set.

1. Go to **Settings | Data Models**.
2. Click on **New Data Model**.
3. In the **Title** type Unicorn Fashion Digital Analytics and click on **Create**. A new data model will be created.
4. Click **Add Object** and choose **Root Event**. There are four types of objects:
    - Event objects — a set of events
    - Transaction objects — transactions and groups of events
    - Search objects — the result of an arbitrary search
    - Child objects — a subset of the dataset connected by their parent object
5. Type in the **Object Name** as Digital Data and **Constraints** as index=digital_analytics sourcetype=access_combined. Click on **Save**:

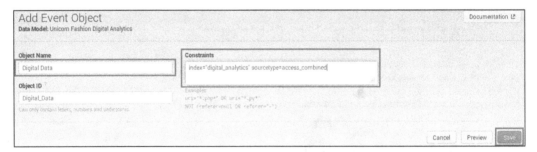

6. Moreover, we can add child events in order to create predefined events with additional constraints.

A **constraint** is a search that defines the dataset that an object represents. It uses root event objects and all child objects to define the dataset that they represent. All child objects inherit constraints from their parent objects, and have a new constraint of their own.

Add auto-extracting fields

We successfully added a root event and now we can add fields that Hunk can extract automatically. Let's do it:

1. Select the **Digital Data** object.

2. Click **Add Attribute** and select **Auto-Extracted**. A new window will come up displaying all auto-extracted fields. Check the checkbox to the left of the **Field** column header in order to select all extracted fields. In addition, we can easily rename some fields.

3. Change the **clientip** type to **IPV4**.

4. Click on **Save**:

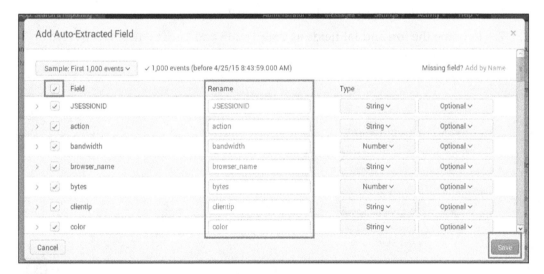

There are four types of attribute in Hunk:

*   **String**: With this, field values are recognized as alpha-numeric.
*   **Number**: With this, field values are recognized as numeric.
*   **Boolean**: With this, field values are recognized as true/false or 1/0.

- **IPV4**: With this, field values are recognized as IP addresses. This field type is useful for geo data because Hunk can easily extract geo data from the IP address.

Moreover, there are also four types of attribute flag:

- **Required**: Only events that contain this field are returned in the pivot
- **Optional**: This field doesn't have to appear in every event
- **Hidden**: This field is not displayed to pivot users when they select an object in the pivot
- **Hidden & Required**: only events that contain this field are returned, and the fields are hidden from use in the pivot

Adding GeoIP attributes

In order to add GeoIP attributes we should have a latitude and longitude lookup table or GeoIP mapping fields.

Let's add GeoIP attributes:

1. Click on **Add Attribute** and choose **GeoIP**.
2. Rename the **lon** and **lat** fields as longitude and latitude respectively. Click on **Save**:

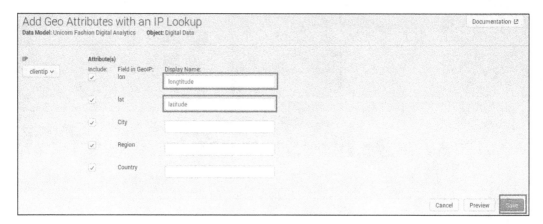

As a result new fields will be added to our data model.

Other ways to add attributes

Hunk offers us other methods of adding attributes, such as:

- **Eval expression**: This allows us to define a new field using an `eval` expression

> For more information about the `eval` expression, see: http://docs.splunk.com/Documentation/Splunk/ latest/Knowledge/Addanevalexpressionattribute.

- **Lookup**: This allows us to use existing lookup definitions to add fields to our event object

> For more information about lookup in data models, see: http://docs.splunk.com/Documentation/Splunk/ latest/Knowledge/Addalookupattribute.

- **Regular expression**: This allows us to define a new field using a regular expression

> For more information about regular expressions in data models, see: http://docs.splunk.com/ Documentation/Splunk/latest/Knowledge/ Addaregularexpressionattribute.

Introducing Pivot

A data model is a semantic layer that makes Hunk a powerful analytical tool for business users. Pivot is a user-friendly interface where anyone can create complex multidimensional reports or interactive dashboards that can be distributed across colleagues.

Let's explore the Pivot UI. Click on **Pivot**, select the **Unicorn Fashion Digital Analytics** data model, and Pivot UI will come up:

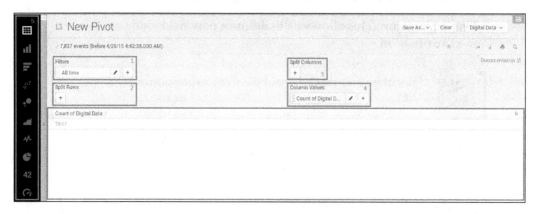

Pivot UI consists of the following main elements:

Pivot element	Definition
Filters (1)	This is used to cut down the result count for the object. There are restrictions in addition to those that might be applied via constraints or other means in the object's definition. All Pivots are filtered by time range. We can optionally add one or more filters by attribute.
Split Rows (2)	This splits out the Pivot results by row. For example, we could use this element to configure a page view object to display a row for each month of the past year, thus breaking out the page view count by month.
Split Columns (3)	This breaks out field values by column. For example, we could design a Pivot table for a page view event-based object that breaks out its returned events by the page_category of the pages viewed (product information, blog, store, support, and so on).
Column Values (4)	This is usually numeric in nature and represents aggregates such as result counts, sums, and averages (in the case of non-numeric attributes you can do things such as listing distinct attribute values). When we first enter a Pivot table, we find a default column value element that uses the Count of <name of object> attribute.
Data visualization tab (5)	This tab has various chart data visualizations for exploring our data. They are: Table, Column chart, Bar chart, Scatter chart, Area chart, Line chart, Pie chart, Single value visualization, Radial gauge, Marker gauge, and Filler gauge.
Result tab (6)	This tab represents the final result of the Pivot editor that can be saved as a report or dashboard.

In order to successfully finish this chapter in style, let's create a chart via Pivot and try to look at brands by categories:

1. Choose **Column Chart** in the **Data Visualization** tab.

2. In **Filter** choose **status | 300** in order to choose only successful transactions.

3. In the **X-Axis** choose the **productBrand** as **Field** and type `Brand` in **Label**. Change **Label Rotation** to **-45**.

4. In the **Y-Axis** leave the default **Count of Digital Data** and type `Count` in **Label**.

5. In **Color** choose **productName** as the **Field** and choose **Stack Mode** as **stacked**. Change **Legend Positions** to **Top**.

6. Click on **Save as Report** and name the report: `Brands by Categories`.

7. Go to the **Reports** tab and open the new report:

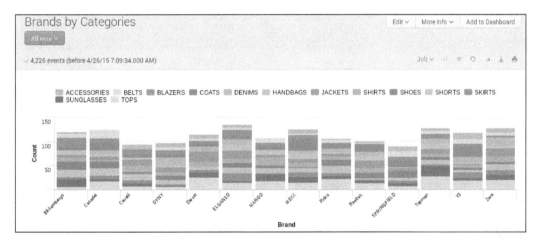

We have successfully created a report via Pivot and learned how to explore data with a user-friendly interface.

Summary

In this chapter, we learnt about extended Hunk features such as knowledge objects. They give additional power to Hunk users during big data analytics. We learnt how to create a semantic layer and work with Pivot. In addition, we explored field aliases and learnt how to extract new fields or calculate them.

In the next chapter, we are going to explore Hunk's report acceleration feature, which can be very useful for getting business insights from big data very quickly.

4

Adding Speed to Reports

One of the attributes of big data analytics is its velocity. In the modern world of information technology, speed is one of the crucial factors of any successful organization because even delays measured in seconds can cost money. Big data must move at extremely high velocities no matter how much we scale or what workloads our store must handle. The data handling hoops of Hadoop or NoSQL solutions put a serious drag on performance. That's why Hunk has a powerful feature that can speed up analytics and help immediately derive business insight from a vast amount of data.

In this chapter, we will learn about the report acceleration technique of Hunk, create new virtual indexes, and compare the performance of the same search with and without acceleration.

Big data performance issues

Despite the fact that, with modern technology, we can handle any big data issue, we still to have spend some time waiting for our questions to be answered. For example, we collect data and store it in Hadoop, then we deploy Hunk and configure a data provider, create a virtual index, and start to ask business questions by creating a query and running search commands. We should wait before the MapReduce job is finished. The following diagram illustrates this situation:

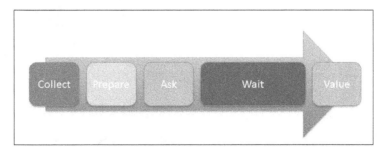

Moreover, if we want to ask the question over and over again by modifying the initial query, we will lose much time and money.

It would be superb if we could just run the search and immediately get the answer, as in the following diagram:

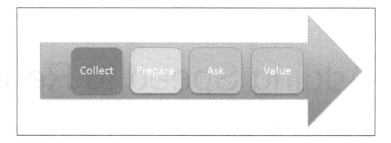

Yes, this is possible with Hunk, because it allows us to accelerate the report and get an answer to our business question very quickly. Let's learn how to do it.

Hunk report acceleration

We can easily accelerate our searches, which is critical for business. The idea behind Hunk is easy: the same search on the same data always gives the same result. In other words, same search + same data = same results. In the case of acceleration, Hunk caches the results and returns them on demand. Moreover, it gives us the opportunity to choose a data range for a particular data summary. In other words, if the data change is due to a fresh portion of events, then the accelerated report will rebuild the data summary in order to meet the requirements of the particular data range. Technically, we just cache the map phase in HDFS. When we run the accelerated search, Hunk just returns straight to us. There are four main steps in running an accelerated search:

1. The scheduled job builds a cache.
2. Find cache hits.
3. Stream the results to a search head.
4. Reduce on the search head.

 There is more information about search heads at:
`http://docs.splunk.com/Splexicon:Searchhead.`

The acceleration feature gives us lots of benefits, such as fast reports on unstructured data as well as on structured data. In addition, we can create fast dashboards and reports. As a result, it helps to improve user experience. Moreover, if we cache the result for mappers, then we just return it streaming to the search head and no mappers will work. It helps to reduce resources.

Creating a virtual index

Let's create a new index based on fake data in order to learn about report acceleration:

1. Go to **Settings | Virtual indexes**.

2. Click on **New virtual index**.

3. Enter orders in the **Name** field.

4. Enter /staging/orders in **Path to data in HDFS** field and click on **Save**:

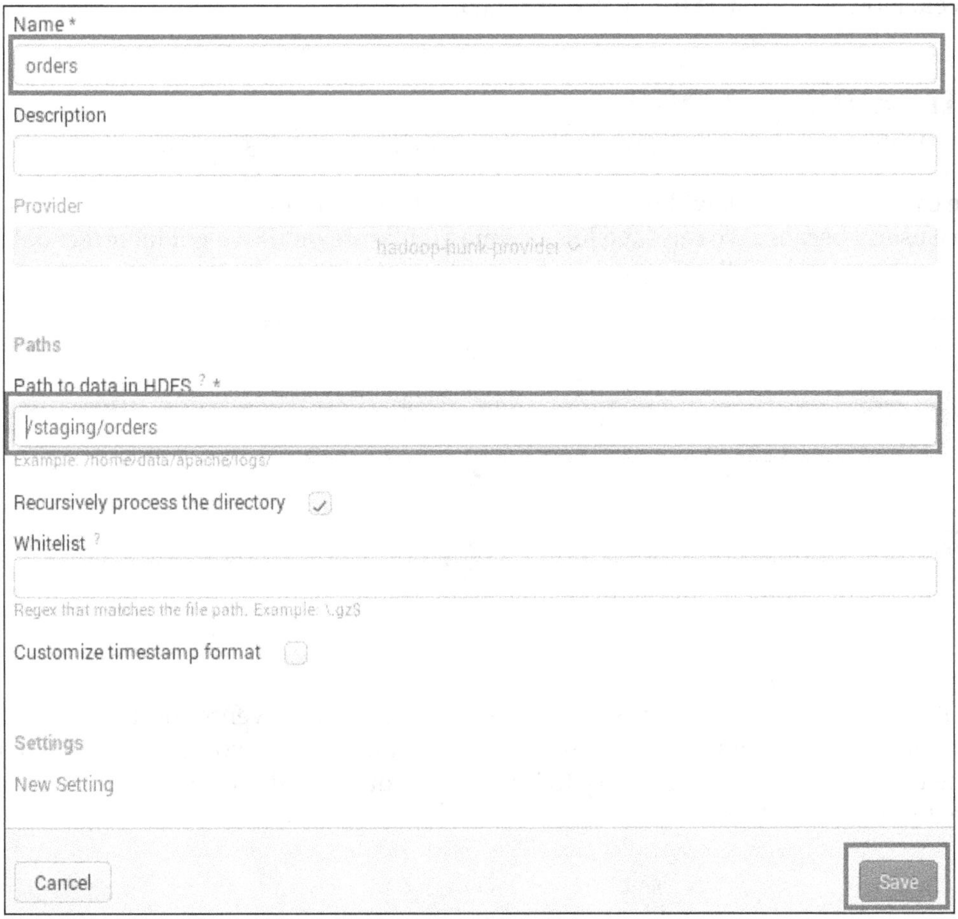

Name *

> orders

Description

Provider

> hadoop-hunk-provider ▾

Paths

Path to data in HDFS ? *

> /staging/orders

Example: /home/data/apache/logs/

Recursively process the directory ☑

Whitelist ?

Regex that matches the file path. Example: \.gz$

Customize timestamp format ☐

Settings

New Setting

Cancel   Save

5. Then we can start to explore the data; click on **Explore Data**.

6. Select **hadoop-Hunk-provider** and **Virtual index** in the **Provider** and **Orders** fields respectively. Click on **Next**.

7. Select the `orders.txt` file and click on **Next**.

8. In **Preview data**, we should choose the appropriate source type or create our own. By default, Hunk can't find the timestamp in our data set. We should try to help it to identify the timestamp.

9. Click on **Timestamp** and enter `timestamp` in the **Timestamp prefix** field; Hunk will define events in our data set. Then click on **Save As** and type the **Sourcetype** name as `onlineorders`. In addition, choose the default app as **Search and Reporting**. Then click on **Next**.

10. In the application context, choose **Search**, click on **Next,** and then click **Finish**.

We got a message from Hunk to the effect that our new configuration has been saved. Now we can start to explore our data.

Streaming mode

Let's look at events from our new index. Just run a search: `index="orders"`.

We can see how Hunk will return events until the map reduce phase finishes. It is very useful because we can save lots of time and figure out if we got incorrect data at the beginning. The following screenshot explains this:

At the beginning, Hunk returns 12,347 events from 118,544 events and then continues to return other events. That's how streaming mode works but it takes some time to achieve the result. Let's try to build a new query and accelerate it in order to see this incredible feature.

Creating an acceleration search

Let's create another search that returns the top category from index orders:

```
index="orders" | top "items{}.category" | rename "items{}.category" as
Category | sort -Category | eval message = "Hello World"
```

It looks silly; however it works more than a minute on my laptop. Save as **Report |
Top Category**.

 In order to accelerate a report, a report must have an underlying
search that uses a transforming command (such as `chart`,
`timechart`, `stats`, and `top`). In addition, any search
commands before the first transforming command in the
search string need to be streaming commands. (Nonstreaming
commands are allowed after the first transforming command.)

Now we can accelerate this report:

1. Go to **Reports** in **Search App**.

2. Click on **Edit** in the **Actions** column and click on **Edit Acceleration**:

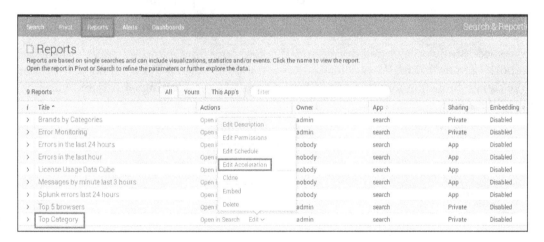

3. A new window — **Edit Acceleration** — will appear.

4. Check **Accelerate Report**, choose **Summary Range | All Time**, and click on **Save**:

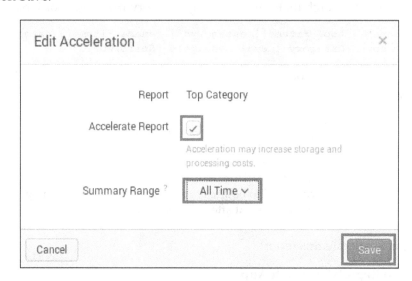

 When we enable acceleration for our report, Hunk will begin to build a report acceleration summary for it.

We successfully accelerated our report. It takes some time in order to accelerate a report. Let's try to run the accelerated report; it takes around 7 seconds on my laptop. We can go to the job monitor and compare results. Go to **Settings | Job** and verify the differences:

In my case, it is 7 seconds versus 1 minute and 27 seconds.

It's an amazing result. Let's try to understand how to manage report acceleration and review our acceleration reports.

What's going on in Hadoop?

As we learnt before, after the map phase, a cache is created in HDFS. We can be more precise: `<vix.splunk.home.hdfs>/cache`. If you are interested in where the cache storing is, then we can use Hue in order to look at the file system. We should open the Hue job browser (`https://quickstart.cloudera:8888/jobbrowser/`) and find the job, which begins from `SPLK_quickstart.cloudera_scheduler__admin__search`. If we start looking at the logs we can find a trace of cache as follows:

```
015-04-29 14:05:24,256 INFO [main] com.splunk.mr.SplunkBaseMapper: Pushed records=118544, bytes=116267468 to search process ...
```

```
2015-04-29 14:05:25,245 INFO [main] com.splunk.mr.SplunkSearchMapper: Processed records=118544, bytes=116267468, return_code=0, elapsed_ms=10078
```

In other words, all things are going in Hadoop.

Report acceleration summaries

When we have created the accelerated search, we can go to the menu, where we can find our acceleration searches and their statistics. In order to find this menu, click on **Settings | Report Acceleration Summaries**:

Summary ID ‡	Normalized Summary ID ‡	Reports Using Summary	Summarization Load ‡ ⊚	Access Count ‡	Summary Status ‡
Showing 1-2 of 2 items					Results per page 25 ▾
01R012ZE107ebe6	N00c17s905TJbf72ce	Top Category	0.1012	0 Last Access Never	Complete Updated 5h ago
018af18ea8627c18	H900aa7bbSh48cc9f2	1	0.0902	0 Last Access Never	Complete Updated 5m ago
Showing 1-2 of 2 items					

> There is more information about report acceleration summaries at: `http://docs.splunk.com/Documentation/Splunk/6.2.5/Knowledge/Manageacceleratedsearchsummaries#Review_summary_details`.

Here we can see common information about report summaries. Let's learn more about the names of the columns:

Name of Column	Definition
Summary ID	The unique hashes that Hunk assigns to summaries.
Normalized Summary ID	The IDs are derived from the remote search string for the report. They are used as part of the directory name that Hunk creates for the summary files.
Report Using Summary	The name of the report.

Name of Column	Definition
Summarization Load	This is calculated by dividing the number of seconds it takes to run the populating report by the interval of the populating report.
Access Count	This shows whether the summary is rarely used or hasn't been used in a long time.
Summary Status	This is the general state of the summary and tells you when it was last updated with new data. Possible status values are complete, pending, suspended, not enough data to summarize, or the percentage of the summary that is complete at the moment.

If we need summary details or we want to perform summary management actions, we should click on a summary ID or normalized summary ID to view summary details.

Reviewing summary details

Let's click on one of the IDs in our summary for the top categories:

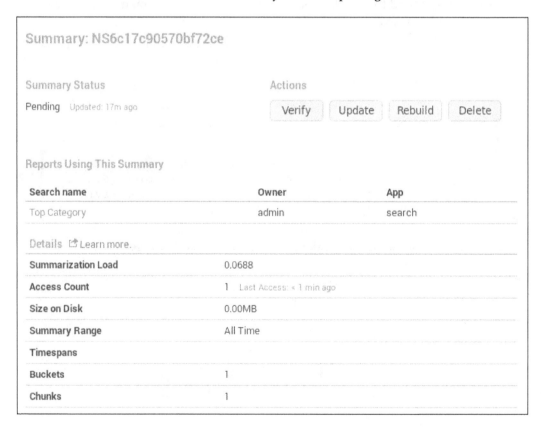

Under **Summary Status**, we can see the status information for the summary. It has the same information as the previous menu, but it also provides information about the verification status of the summary. As a result, we can easily update a summary to the present moment by clicking **Update** to kick off a new summary-populating report.

 If the Size value stays at 0.00 MB it means that Hunk is not currently generating this summary because the reports associated with it either don't have enough events (at least 100k hot bucket events are required) or the projected summary size is over 10 percent of the bucket with which the report is associated. Hunk will periodically check this report and automatically create a summary for it when it meets the criteria for summary creation. But, anyway, our search starts to work faster.

Managing report accelerations

The report acceleration files for the Hadoop ERP are stored in HDFS. By default we can find files in `<vix.splunk.home.hdfs>/cache`. Let's check it via Hue.

Go to Hue `http://quickstart.cloudera:8888/filebrowser/` and click on **File Browser**. Go to **user | hunk | cache**:

Here we can find a file that has information about the cache. Go to **orders** and find `info.json`, which has information about our summary:

```
{"index":"orders","search":"search (index=orders) | addinfo type=count
label=prereport_events | fields keepcolorder=t \"cvp_reserved_count\"
\"items{}.category\" | pretop 10 \"items{}.category\"","summary_
id":"D2DB9B94-7D5E-47B2-B9F9-D419A67CAC05_search_admin_
NS6c17c90570bf72ce"}
```

Hunk accelerations limits

Hunk is superb, but it still has some drawbacks:

- Hardware limitations related to memory consumption by the search head. They are solved by adjusting the memory configuration.

- Software limitations related to the cache. Sometimes we should delete the old cache using command `rm -rf <vix.splunk.home.hdfs>/cash`.

- Human factor — this is a popular issue, especially in analytics. We learnt that, for Hunk, acceleration means: same search + same data = same result. But it won't work if we change the KV extraction rules. Be careful with this.

Summary

In this chapter we learnt how to accelerate searches in Hunk. This feature is easy to use and maintain. It helps to reduce resources and improve user experience. In addition, we learnt how acceleration works and created our own accelerated report. Moreover, we compared it with a normal report and figured out how it became faster. Finally, we learnt how to manage Hunk report summaries.

We also learnt much about the base functionality of Hunk. In the next chapter, we are going to extend Hunk functionality via Hunk SDK and Rest API.

5
Customizing Hunk

Splunk has a rich SDK that allows you to create custom dashboards with extended functionality. The aim of this chapter is to show you how to create a custom dashboard using data stored in Hadoop. We are going to visualize data containing aggregated customer data records on Google Maps. The goal is to show a customer activity heatmap.

What we are going to do with the Splunk SDK

Splunk has various SDKs for different languages and platforms. We are going to talk about them shortly and won't cover deep application development. Our goal is to get the result as rapidly as possible and using few application development skills. We can always turn to custom development, and our goal is to get quick insights as soon as possible.

There is a nice portal—https://splunkbase.splunk.com—where you can find hundreds of published applications. Extending Splunk with a SDK is not something special; it's a recommended approach to get extended functionality. This book has a chapter describing integration with MongoDB. The MongoDB integration application is taken from the splunkbase portal. We encourage you to look through published apps before starting to develop your own.

Supported languages

You can use several languages to create custom applications for Splunk:

- Python
- Java

- JavaScript
- PHP
- Ruby
- C#

Great, we have a set of popular languages; it shouldn't be a problem to find guys who knows a least one of the listed languages.

Solving problems

Splunk SDK could be used for these purposes:

- Integrating with third-party software
- Logging directly to Splunk
- Running search queries and getting results to display in your custom application
- Building custom UIs and other features

REST API

Splunk provides a REST API for its services. Generally, it means that you can interact with Splunk components using `curl/wget` or any other tool or language library that can send a correct HTTP request. Splunk provides so-called endpoints for services. You can call Splunk using a GET request:

```
search/jobs/export
```

To stream search results. Any Splunk component has its own endpoint. The Splunk SDK for the languages listed earlier simplifies interaction with the service endpoints. Each language SDK provides bindings for API endpoints and a level of abstraction over HTTP calls. This approach is common; for example, Cloudera manager API provides a Java and Python SDK. These SDKs are just wrappers for REST services of Cloudera manager. The good point is that you can integrate with Splunk and you don't have to be tightly coupled with Ruby or C#, for example. You can even call services using C++.

The implementation plan

We are going to cover these topics in order to develop a custom dashboard with heatmaps based on aggregated customer data records collected in Milano, Italy:

- Learn how raw data looks like and what properties it has

- Create a data sample using Pig to make development iteration shorter

- Query our data using Splunk's query language to see if data presented correctly and the query returns the expected results

- Meet the Splunk JS SDK API to extend basic functionality in Splunk and visualize the heatmap results

The conclusion

Application development using Splunk SDK would make a separate book, which is why we only touch on it briefly here. Let's summarize the good points:

- Splunk provides access from various popular languages.

- Splunk services have endpoints and we can reach them using the REST API with the help of `curl/wget` or any other tool that sends HTTP requests.

- SDK wraps the REST API internally to simplify interaction with Splunk services. It would be the best choice for production implementation.

Now it's time to move on to dashboard visualization using the Splunk JS stack. This should help us to reach our goal: getting results using minimal application development skills.

Dashboard customization using Splunk Web Framework

We have discovered many different dashboards created using the default Hunk functionality. Now it's time to create our own dashboard with unique functionality using the Splunk JS SDK API (JavaScript).

Functionality

We are going to use the Splunk JS API to customize our map visualization and create input controls.

We will cover these functions:

- Extending an existing map component and making it display rectangles

- Configuring input controls to modify search queries and display different data dimensions: incoming, outgoing SMS activity, and so on

A description of time-series aggregated CDR data

We used the Oozie coordinator in *Chapter 1, Meet Hunk,* to import *massive* amounts of data. Data is partitioned by date and stored in binary format with a schema. It looks like a production-ready approach. Avro is pretty well supported across the whole Hadoop ecosystem. Now we are going to create a custom application using that data. Have a look at the description of the data.

Here is a description of the data stored in the base table:

- **Square ID**: The ID of the square that is part of the Milano grid type: numeric.
- **Time interval**: The beginning of the time interval expressed as the number of milliseconds elapsed from the Unix Epoch on January 1, 1970 at UTC. The end of the time interval can be obtained by adding 600,000 milliseconds (10 minutes) to this value.
- **Country code**: The phone code of a nation. Depending on the measured activity this value assumes different meanings that are explained later.
- **SMS-in activity**: The activity in terms of received SMS inside the square ID, during the time interval and sent from the nation identified by the country code.
- **SMS-out activity**: The activity in terms of sent SMS inside the square ID, during the time interval and received by the nation identified by the country code.
- **Call-in activity**: The activity in terms of received calls inside the square ID, during the time interval and issued from the nation identified by the country code.
- **Call-out activity**: The activity in terms of issued calls inside the square ID, during the time interval and received by the nation identified by the country code.
- **Internet traffic activity**: The activity in terms of Internet traffic performed inside the square ID, during the time interval and by the nation of the users performing the connection identified by the country code.

The following screenshot is from the site hosting the dataset:

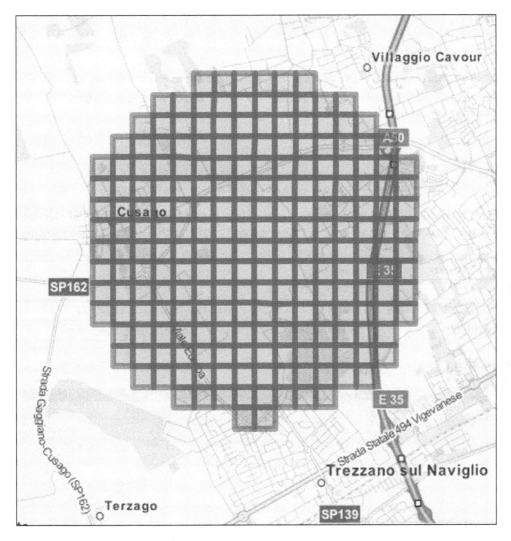

The idea of this dataset is to divide the city in to equal areas and map the typed subscriber activity on these regions. The assumption is that such mapping can give insights about relations between the hour of the day, type of activity, and area of the city.

Source data

There are two datasets. The first one contains customer activity (CDR). The second dataset looks like a dictionary. It has exact coordinates for each *activity square* represented in the earlier screenshot.

Creating a virtual index for Milano CDR

You should refer to the section *Setting up virtual index for data stored in Hadoop* in *Chapter 2, Explore Hadoop Data with Hunk*. Virtual index creation for Milano CDR is there. You have the CDR layout in HDFS:

```
[cloudera@quickstart ~]$ hadoop fs -ls -R /masterdata/stream/milano_cdr
drwxr-xr-x   - cloudera supergroup          0 2015-08-03 13:55 /
masterdata/stream/milano_cdr/2013
drwxr-xr-x   - cloudera supergroup          0 2015-03-25 02:13
some output deleted to reduce size of it.
-rw-r--r--   1 cloudera supergroup   69259863 2015-03-25 02:13 /
masterdata/stream/milano_cdr/2013/12/07/part-m-00000.avro
```

So you have relatively compact aggregated data for the first seven days of December 2013. Let's create a virtual index for December 1, 2013. It should have these settings:

Property name	Value
Name	`Milano_2013_12_01`
Path to data in HDFS	`/masterdata/stream/milano_cdr/2013/12/01`
Provider	Choose Hadoop hunk provider from the dropdown list

Explore it and check that you see this sample data:

Creating a virtual index for the Milano grid

There is a file that provides longitude and latitude values for squares. We need to create a virtual index on top of this dictionary, to be joined later with the aggregated data. We need actual coordinates to display squares on Google Maps.

Virtual index settings for the so-called `geojson` should be:

Property name	Value
Name	`geojson`
Path to data in HDFS	`/masterdata/dict/milano_cdr_grid_csv`
Provider	Choose Hadoop hunk provider from the dropdown list

Let's try to explore some data from that virtual index:

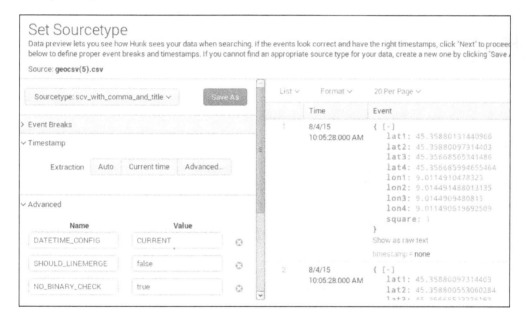

You have to scroll down and verify the advanced settings for the index. The names and values should be:

Property name	Value
Name	geojson
DATETIME_CONFIG	CURRENT
SHOULD_LINEMERGE	False
NO_BINARY_CHECK	True
disabled	False
pulldown_type	True

Save the settings with this name: scv_with_comma_and_title.

Verify that you can see lines with longitude, latitude, and squares.

Use the search application to verify that the virtual index is set correctly. Here is a search query; it selects several fields from the index:

```
index="geojson" | fields square, lon1,lat1 | head 10
```

The following screenshot shows the sample output:

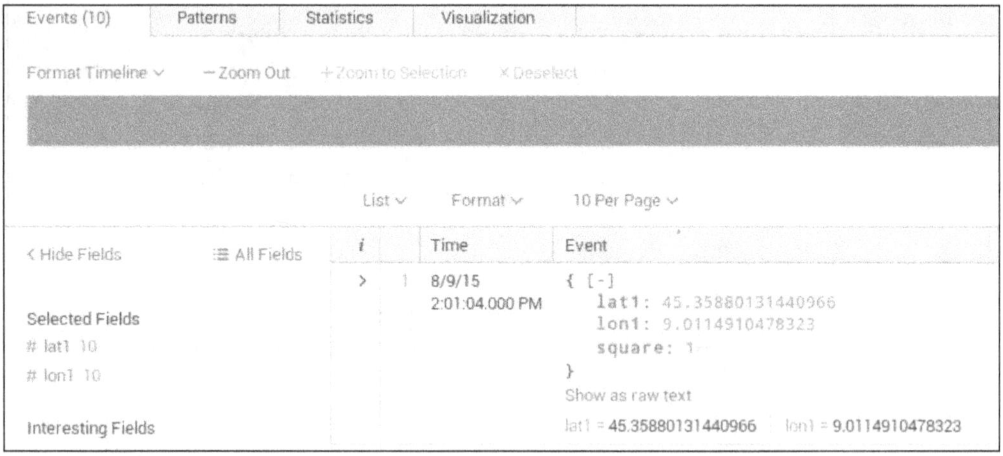

Creating a virtual index using sample data

We would like to shorten the feedback loop while developing our application. Let's trim the source data so our queries work faster.

You need to open the Pig editor `http://quickstart.cloudera:8888/ pig/#scripts` and open the script stored there:

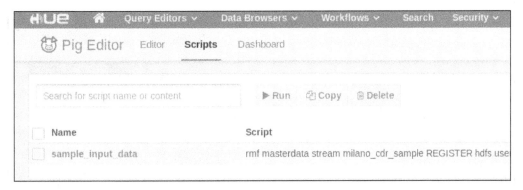

Then you should see the script. Click the **Submit** button to run the script and create a sample dataset:

- **--remove output path**: We need clean output path before script execution:

  ```
  rmf /masterdata/stream/milano_cdr_sample
  ```

- **--add jar used by AvroStorage**: It's a Pig storage implementation for reading avro data:

  ```
  REGISTER 'hdfs:///user/oozie/share/lib/lib_20141218043440/sqoop/
  avro-mapred-1.7.6-cdh5.3.0-hadoop2.jar'
  ```

- **--read input data**:

  ```
  data = LOAD '/masterdata/stream/milano_cdr/2013/12/01' using
  AvroStorage();
  ```

- **--filter**: To filter out all lines except lines where `time_interval` is equal to `1385884800000L`:

  ```
  filtered = FILTER data by time_interval ==  1385884800000L;
  ```

- **--store filtered data**:

  ```
  store filtered into '/masterdata/stream/milano_cdr_sample' using
  AvroStorage();
  ```

Have a look at the HUE UI. This is an editor for Pig scripts. You should find a ready-to-use script on the VM. The only thing you need to do is click the **Submit** button:

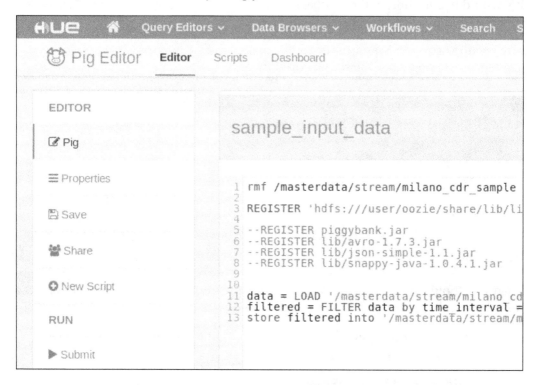

This script reads the first day of the dataset and filters it by using the time_interval field. This approach significantly reduces the amount of data. You should get the output in a few minutes:

```
Input(s):
```

```
Successfully read 4637377 records (91757807 bytes) from: "/masterdata/
stream/milano_cdr/2013/12/01"
```

```
Output(s):
```

```
Successfully stored 35473 records (2093830 bytes) in: "/masterdata/
stream/milano_cdr_sample"
```

```
Counters:
```

```
Total records written : 35473
```

```
Total bytes written : 2093830
```

```
Spillable Memory Manager spill count : 0
```

```
Total bags proactively spilled: 0
Total records proactively spilled: 0
```

There will be more lines in output; just try to find the ones we've mentioned. They say that Pig reads 4.6 million records and stores 35 thousand records. We reduced the amount of data for testing purposes, as described earlier.

Now create a virtual index over the sample data; we can use it while developing our application. Here are the settings; use these to facilitate development:

Property name	Value
Name	`milano_cdr_sample`
Path to data in HDFS	`/masterdata/stream/milano_cdr_sample`
Provider	Choose Hadoop hunk provider from the dropdown list

Use the search application to check so that you can correctly access the sample data:

```
index="milano_cdr_sample" | head 10
```

You should see something similar to this:

Implementation

Now it's time to implement heatmap application. We will start from creating query to get sample data for application and then move forward to coding visualization using Javascript and Python.

Querying the visualization

Let us start to get acquainted with the data we have. We are going to explore sample data to make the process faster.

We are going to use the next query during development. We will display a heatmap for the center of Milano. The other simplification is a hardcoded time interval. We removed all other intervals from the sample dataset using the Pig script earlier. The general idea is to reduce the amount of data and make the development cycle shorter:

```
(index="milano_cdr_sample" time_interval=1385884800000
AND (
  (square_id >5540 AND square_id < 5560) OR
  (square_id >5640 AND square_id < 5660) OR
  (square_id >5740 AND square_id < 5760)
  )
)

| fields square_id, sms_in, time_interval

| stats sum(sms_in) as cdrActivityValue by square_id, time_interval

| join square_id

[search

(index ="geojson"
  (square >5540 AND square < 5560) OR
  (square >5640 AND square < 5660) OR
  (square >5740 AND square < 5760)
)

| fields square, lon1, lat1, lon3, lat3
| rename square as square_id]
| fields cdrActivityValue, lon1, lat1, lon3, lat3
|head 10
```

The query flow is:

- Read data from the `Milano_cdr_sample` index, and filter by `time_interval` (December 1, 2013, early morning) and `square_id` while reading the data.

- Sum the `sms_in` value while grouping by `square_id` and `time_interval`. Country code field is omitted for simplification purposes. We get `sms_in` activity for each Milano city square after completing the group operation.

- We need to get longitude and latitude for each `square_id`, stored in `Milano_cdr_example_index`. We use a join operation to join the index named `geojson`. The second index contains longitudes and latitudes for squares. We need the top left and bottom right angles to display a rectangle on the map using the Google Maps API. That's why we select `lon1`, `lat1`, `lon3`, and `lat3`.

- Then we project the fields we need.

- `| head 10` returns the first 10 results. We are going to remove this pipe operation later.

Downloading the application

Visit `http://www.bigdatapath.com/2015/09/customizing-hunk/` and download the application. Untar it locally. Don't be afraid if you see multiple folders and files. They are generated by the SDK framework utility. SDK generated the Django application skeleton. Django framework description is omitted for simplification. We would have to change few files in order to make application solve our problem. We will work with one file located here:

`milanocdr/django/googlemaps/templates/home.html`

Please open chapter related to Mongo integration and see detailed description for application installation process.

Custom Google Maps

Let's have a look at the code. Just search for the highlighted code snippets, to find the relevant discussion point.

Page layout

Find the: `<!-- Page layout -->` comment. You can see the layout for the page.
The layout is simple; pick an activity type and map where the data will be displayed:

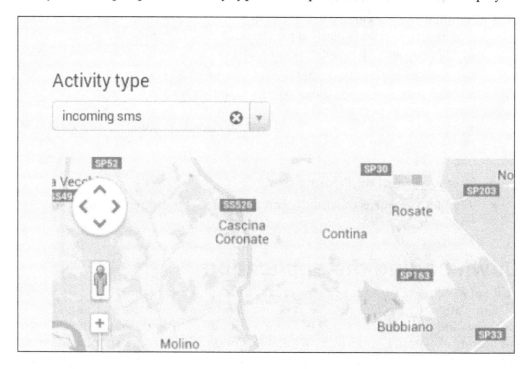

You can see small squares near **Rosate**. These squares are coded by color. Green
denoted the lowest activity and red the highest.

Linear gradients and bins for the activity value

We will use linear gradients for simplicity. You would definitely switch to
logarithmic gradients or linear and logarithmic ones. We don't consider value
amounts for each bean; the idea is just to equally split the difference between the
current mix and max values on five equal ranges:

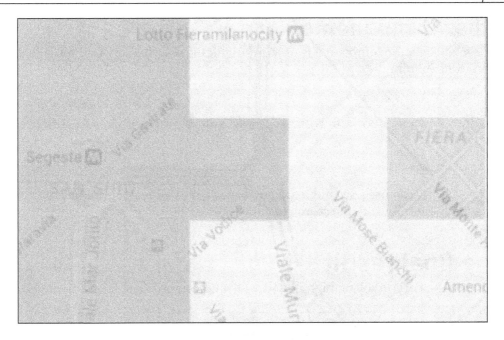

Find `//colors for the values` to see the list of colors for the bins. The first is green, the last is dark red:

```
function assignBinColors(rectangles)
```

The preceding code is responsible for assigning color bins for squares. It uses a simple formula to calculate bin size:

```
var binSize = (max-min) / (binColors.length-1);
```

Custom map components

We change the behavior of the `GoogleMapView` component:

```
var customHeatMap = GoogleMapView.extend
```

The idea is to override the `render` method and provide custom handling for the search result. Each row returned from the search manager is presented as:

```
google.maps.Rectangle
```

Other components

The `SearchManager` component is used to submit the search query and retrieve the result from Splunk:

```
var search = new SearchManager
```

This drop-down input control with predefined values provides access to different types of activity:

```
new DropdownView
```

By the way, we can use a second search manager and populate `DropdownView` content dynamically with the search result.

The final result

You can see a part of Milano highlighted with a heatmap:

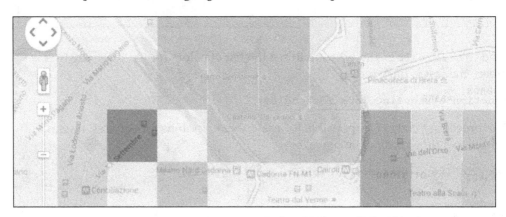

The heatmap displays reasonable data. Low activity is observed in the park areas and high activity near metro stations.

Summary

Splunk provides various approaches for custom application development. It's possible to start with a so-called *simple XML* that provides basic functionality. XML declarations allow us to create custom input forms and even visualizations on Google Maps. When you need more, you can turn to classical application development using various languages. The earlier example explained one approach to extending existing components. With a few lines of custom code we got a simple interactive map based on data stored in Hadoop and presented as a virtual index.

6
Discovering Hunk Integration Apps

Hunk can be used not only for doing analytics on data stored in Hadoop. We will discover other options using special integration applications. These come from the `https://splunkbase.splunk.com/` portal, which has hundreds of published applications. This chapter is devoted to integration schemes between the popular NoSQL document-oriented Mongo and Hunk stores.

What is Mongo?

Mongo is a popular NoSQL solution. There are many pros and cons for using Mongo. It's a great choice when you want to get simple and rather fast persistent key-value storage with a nice JavaScript interface for querying stored data. We recommend you start with Mongo if you don't really need a strict SQL schema and your data volumes are estimated in terabytes. Mongo is amazingly simple compared to the whole Hadoop ecosystem; probably it's the right option to start exploring the denormalized NoSQL world.

Installation

Mongo is already installed and ready to use. Mongo installation is not described. We use Mongo version 3.0.

You will install the special Hunk app that integrates Mongo and Hunk.

Installing the Mongo app

Visit https://splunkbase.splunk.com/app/1810/#/documentation and download the app. You should use the VM browser to download it:

1. Click on **Splunk Apps**:

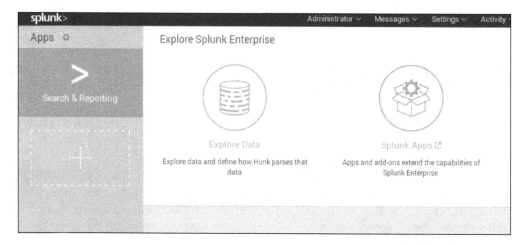

2. Click on **Manage Apps**:

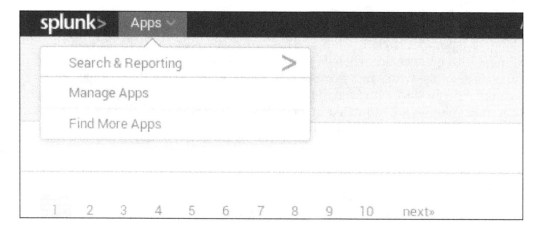

3. Choose **Install app from file**:

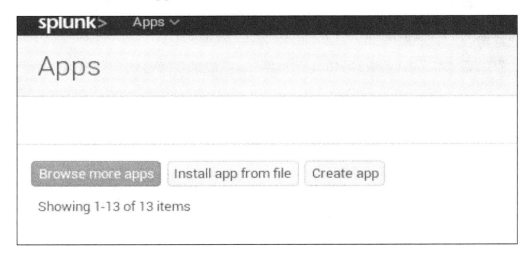

4. Select the downloaded app and install it.

5. You should see the Mongo app among the other installed apps, if successful:

Mongo provider

A Mongo provider is created and used to access Mongo data. Go to the **Virtual Indexes** tab and see the created `local-mongodb` provider:

Check the provider settings:

You can change the property named **vix.mongodb.host** if you want to connect to some other Mongo instance.

Creating a virtual index

Now it's time to create virtual indexes based on Mongo collections. There is a bug.
So you have to:

1. Choose the **hadoop** provider.
2. Change the input path to **Path to data in HDFS**:

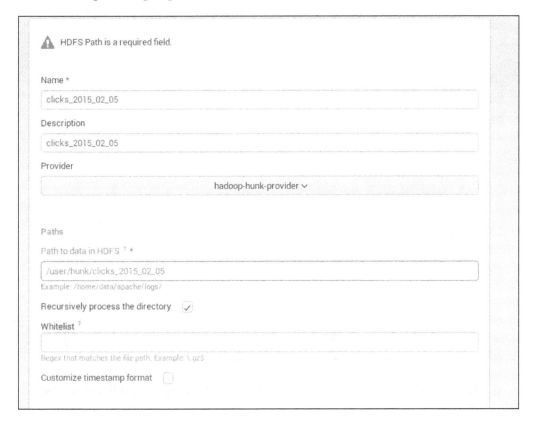

3. Switch back to the `mongo` provider:

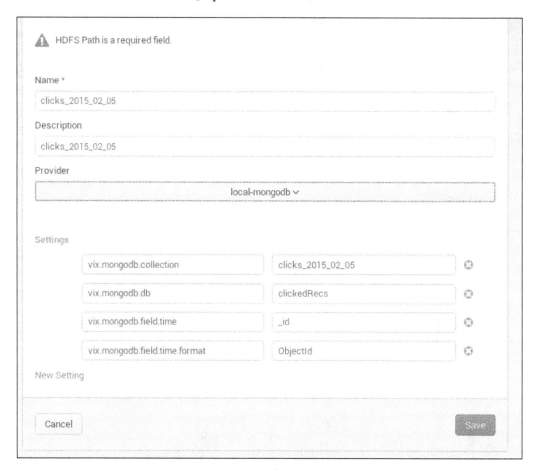

4. Repeat these steps for five mongo collections in order to get five indexes in Hunk:

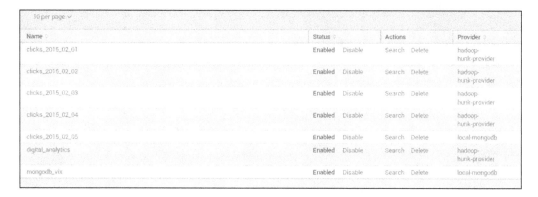

Inputting data from the recommendation engine backend

There is a sample of data collected by the recommendation engine backend. When the user clicks on the recommendation, the event is recorded and sent to Mongo. That data is used to self-tune the recommendation engine later. Data is stored into daily collections. Mongo allows us to create daily collections easily and helps to partition the data. The best approach is to think about data partitioning in advance.

Data schemas

Let's explore data schemas. The schema describes the *document* stored in MongoDB and extracted to Hadoop:

```
{ [-]
    _timestamp: 1423080002
    block_id: 4
    cross_id: 896bba91c21c620b0902fbec05b3246bce21859c
    idvisitor: 783852c991fbefb8
    is_napoleon: 2
    original_id: null
    rec: 2291655
    service: 2
    shop_id: 173
    target_site_id: 0
    time: 1423080002
    type: 1
}
```

We are interested in these fields:

- `timestamp`: When the recommendation click event happened
- `shop_id`: Where the recommendation has been displayed
- `service`: Which service provided the recommendation

Data mechanics

Lets see how data in being generated. There is a user that comes to e-commerce site. His browser gets cookie named `cross_id`. Cookie gives us a chance to track user interaction with site: what pages he visits, what items he clicks. There is a service that shows recommendations to user based on user site activity. Each recommendation has unique ID `rec_id`. Service stores list of recommendations that were displayed to user. Service captures `click` event, when user clicked promoted item from recommendations set. We know exactly which recommendations (with unique key named `rec_id`) did user see and click.

Counting by shop in a single collection

We want to see the number of clicks during the day for each shop.

Use this expression to get the result:

```
index=clicks_2015_02_01 | stats count by shop_id
```

We see that the `shop_id` with ID 173 has the most clicks. I'll let you in on a secret: this shop has many more visitors than the others:

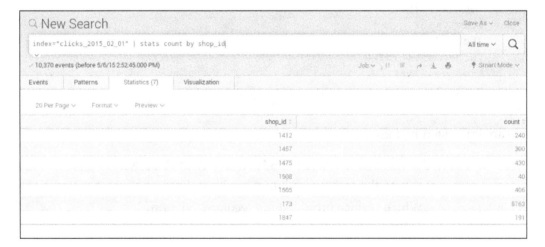

Counting events in all collections

We can access our daily data stored in separated collections and virtual indexes using a pattern. Let's count the events in each collection and sort by the collection size:

Use this expression:

```
index=clicks_2015_* | stats count by index | sort - count
```

We can see the trend: users visit shops during working days more often (the 1st of February is Sunday, the 5th is Thursday) so we get more clicks from them:

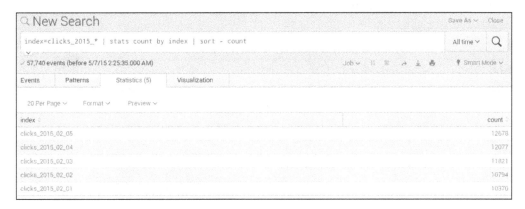

Next is the query related to metadata. We don't query the exact index; we use a wildcard to query several indexes at once:

```
index=clicks_2015_*
```

> Metadata is data that describes data. Index name is the data description. We have virtual indexes based on Mongo collections that hold click events. Each virtual index has a name. So the virtual index name is metadata.

Counting events in shops for observed days

Let's count how many events happen during observed days in each shop:

```
index=clicks_2015_* | stats count by index, shop_id | sort +index,
-count
```

We sort by index name (the lexicographical order will be used) and by the count of events in shops in descending order.

Let's add some formatting to our report:

```
index=clicks_2015_* | eval day = strftime(timestamp, "%Y.%m.%d") |
stats count by shop_id, day | sort +day, -count | fields day, shop_
id, count
```

We want to see the count of clicks in the shops by day:

- We add a field named day and formatted with a timestamp field: `eval day = strftime(timestamp, "%Y.%m.%d")`

- We count the events in each shop by day: `stats count by shop_id, day`

- We order by day, and count: `sort +day, -count`:

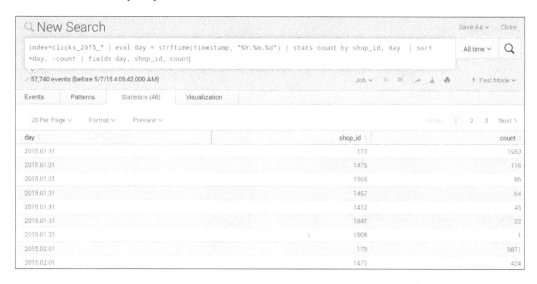

Summary

We learned how to connect to MongoDB and create virtual indexes based on Mongo collections. We got examples of data partitioning on the Mongo side and had run queries touching several partitions represented as virtual indexes on the Hunk side.

7
Exploring Data in the Cloud

Hadoop on the cloud is a new deployment option that allows organizations to create and customize Hadoop clusters on virtual machines utilizing the computing resources of virtual instances and deployment scripts. Similar to the on-premise full custom option, this gives businesses full control of the cluster. In addition, it gives flexibility and many advantages—for example, capacity on demand, decreased staff costs, storage services, and technical support. Finally, it gives the opportunity to get fast time to value, that is we can deploy our infrastructure in the Amazon cloud and start analyze our data very quickly because we don't need setup hardware and software as well as we don't need many technical resources. One of the most popular Hadoop cloud is Amazon **Elastic MapReduce** (**EMR**).

With Hunk we can interactively explore, analyze, and visualize data stored in Amazon EMR and Amazon S3. The integrated offering lets AWS and Splunk customers:

- Unlock the business value of data: Preview search results before MapReduce jobs finish and conduct sophisticated analytics—all from an integrated analytics platform that's fast and easy for everyone to use.

- Gain insights: Hunk lets us explore, analyze, and visualize Amazon EMR and Amazon S3 data on a massive scale, all with just a few clicks.

- Easily provision and deploy Hunk, when we need it, for only as long as you need it—charged by the hour.

In this chapter, the reader will learn how to run Amazon EMR and deploy Hunk on top of it. In addition, the reader will create virtual indexes and use the Amazon S3 file system.

An introduction to Amazon EMR and S3

In this section, we will learn about Amazon EMR and **Simple Storage Service** (**S3**). Moreover, we try to run these services by creating EMR clusters and S3 buckets.

Amazon EMR

Amazon EMR is a Hadoop framework in the cloud offered as a managed service. It is used by thousands of customers. It uses millions of EMR clusters in a variety of big data use cases, including log analysis, web indexing, data warehousing, machine learning, financial analysis, scientific simulation, and bioinformatics. EMR can easily process any type of big data without its own big data infrastructure:

As with any other Amazon service, EMR is easy to run by filling in option forms. Enter the cluster name, the size, and the types of node in the cluster. And it creates in two minutes a fully running EMR cluster. It is ready to process data. It removes all the headache of maintaining clusters and version compatibility. Amazon takes care of all tasks involved in running and supporting Hadoop.

Setting up an Amazon EMR cluster

Let's start EMR cluster in order to connect to Hunk:

1. Go to http://aws.amazon.com and sign up or sign in.
2. Go to the **AWS Management Console** and choose **Amazon EMR**.
3. Click **Create Cluster** and choose the appropriate parameters.
4. Type in the **Cluster name**, for example emr-cluster-packtpub. In addition, we can switch off **Logging** and **Termination protection**:

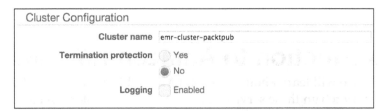

5. Choose a **Hadoop distribution**:

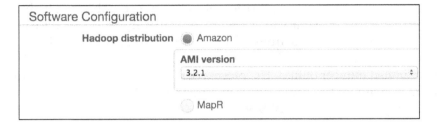

6. Choose an **EC2 instance type** and the number of nodes:

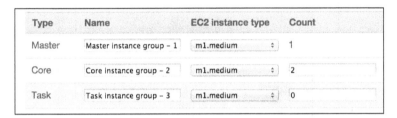

 We can learn more about how to plan the capacity for EMR here:
http://docs.aws.amazon.com/ElasticMapReduce/latest/
DeveloperGuide/emr-plan-instances.html.

If we want to pay for Hunk by the hour, we should add Hunk as an additional application:

7. For **Security and Access**, select your EC2 key pair and IAM user access settings.

8. For **IAM Roles**, select your EMR Role setting and EC2 instance profile for your cluster. Hunk requires that you run your EMR cluster using IAM roles.

9. Click **Create Cluster**. It takes time to prepare and run a new cluster by AWS.

Amazon S3

Amazon S3 provides developers and IT teams with secure, durable, and highly-scalable object storage. Amazon S3 is easy to use, with a simple web service interface to store and retrieve any amount of data from anywhere on the Web. We can easily write and retrieve objects, which can range in size from a few bytes to terabytes, and we can work with an unlimited number of files. The process of interacting with S3 is very trivial, we just use the web service interface to write or retrieve objects. It is reliable, secure, and durable. Finally, it is backed by AWS SLA:

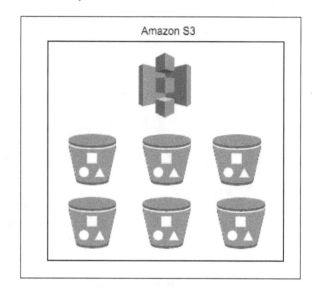

S3 as a data provider for Hunk

Amazon S3 can be a data provider for Hunk. Let's create a bucket and upload two files with two weeks' worth of all HTTP requests to the **ClarkNet WWW** server. ClarkNet is a full Internet access provider for the Metro Baltimore-Washington DC area, and can be found in the attachment to this chapter or as a direct download from: `http://ita.ee.lbl.gov/html/contrib/ClarkNet-HTTP.html`:

1. Go to the AWS Management Console and choose **Amazon S3**.
2. Create a bucket called `my-web-logs`.
3. Choose **Actions** and click **Upload** in order to upload `clarknet_access_log_Aug28` and `clarknet_access_log_Sep4`.
4. When we set up Hunk, we will use this bucket as a data source for a virtual index.

The advantages of EMR and S3

Amazon Elastic MapReduce can be seen as both a complement and a competitor to Hadoop. EMR can run on top of a Hadoop HDFS cluster, but it can also run directly on top of AWS S3. There are several advantages to using S3 and EMR together. First of all, using Amazon EMR and S3 gives us full native support to access data — in other words, we are provided with a full distributed file system and full support from EMR. EMR runs on top of S3 and S3 works as a data store. In addition, it allows us to avoid the complexity of Hadoop and HDFS management. For example, if we have Hadoop on-premise, it is not easy to maintain it:

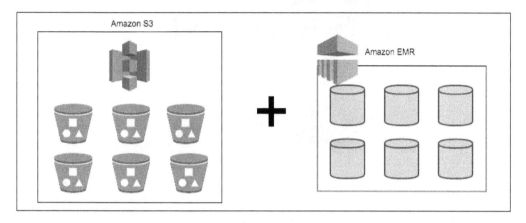

Moreover, EMR is elastic; it is easy to increase clusters dynamically on demand. Finally, it uses a *pay for what you use model*. For example:

- Long running versus Transient
- Spot versus Reserved Instances

Furthermore, EMR and S3 are very popular with thousands of customers; they have a big ecosystem and a very large community.

Integrating Hunk with EMR and S3

Integrating Hunk with EMR and S3 is a pretty sensible proposition. If we connect the vast amounts of data that we store in HDFS or S3 with the rich capabilities of Hunk, we can build a full analytics solution for any type of data and any size of data on the cloud:

Fundamentally, we have a three-tier architecture. The first tier is data storage based on HDFS or S3. The next one is the compute or processing framework, provided by EMR. Finally, the visualization, data discovery, analytics, and app development framework is provided by Hunk.

The traditional method for hosting Hunk in the cloud is to simply buy a standard license and then provision a virtual machine in much the same way you would do it on-site. The instance would then have to be manually configured to point to the correct Hadoop or AWS cluster. This method is also called **Bring Your Own License (BYOL)**.

On the other hand, Splunk and Amazon offer another method, in which Hunk instances can be automatically provisioned in AWS. This includes automatically discovering EMR data sources, which allows for instances to be brought online in a manner of minutes. In order to take advantage of this, Hunk instances are billed at an hourly rate. Let's try to perform both methods.

Method 1: BYOL

We have already run an EMR cluster. In addition, we should load data into S3 or HDFS.

Setting up the Hunk AMI

Let's find and run the Hunk AMI:

1. Go to the AWS Market place — `https://aws.amazon.com/marketplace` — and find the Hunk AMI:

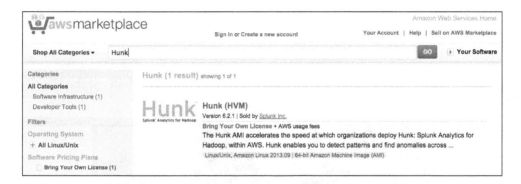

 There is detailed information about Amazon Machine Images at: `http://docs.aws.amazon.com/AWSEC2/latest/UserGuide/AMIs.html`.

2. Choose the appropriate **Instance** depending on your workflow.

 It is important to create an instance with enough resources to accommodate the expected workload and search concurrency. For instance, a `c3.2xlarge` (high-CPU instance) provides a good starting point.

It is important that the Hunk instance can communicate with all EMR cluster nodes. To do this, we have to edit Security Groups in the EC2 Management page to make sure traffic is allowed to and from all ports.

If we are using S3 for our data directories, we have to set up a Hunk working directory in HDFS. This improves processing speed and allows us to keep our directory read-only, if desired.

3. Configure the IAM Role; choose **EC2_EMR_DefaultRole**.
4. Configure the Security Group. Hunk needs to be a part of `ElasticMapReduce-master`. In addition, we should attach to Hunk-Group in order to access the web interface.
5. Click **Launch Instance** and get a new window, where we create a **Key Pair**, or choose the existing one in order to connect the instance by SSH.

As a result, we have a running EMR and Hunk with configured security. We need to copy the **Public DNS**. In the **From EC2** menu, choose our Hunk Instance and copy the **Public DNS**. In addition, we can copy the **Instance ID** as a password for Hunk:

Then paste it in a browser and add `:8000` as a default port. We then get the Hunk Web Interface:

Adding a license

We chose the BYOL model; that's why we should add the license file. Go to **Settings | Licensing** and click on **Add license** in order to upload the license file:

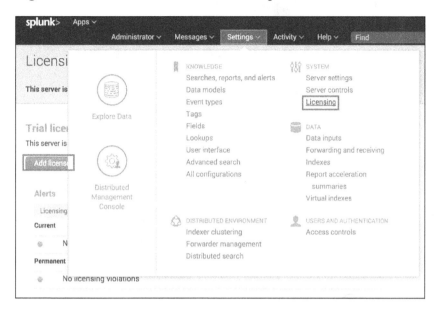

By default we can use the trial license for 60 days.

Configuring the data provider

Let's configure the data provider in order to create a virtual index and start to explore our log file, based on S3:

1. Go to **Settings | Virtual Indexes | Providers** tab and click **New Provider**.

2. Complete the following parameters:

   ° **Name**: Type any name.

   ° **Java Home**: AMI has this default folder: /opt/java/latest/.

   ° **Hadoop Home**: AMI has a default folder for various Hadoop versions: /opt/hadoop/apache/hadoop-X.X.X.

   ° **Hadoop Version**: Choose the appropriate one.

   ° **Job Tracker**: We need to use the Private IP of the Master Node.

   ° **File System**: In the case of S3, we should use this: s3n://<AWS key>:<AWS secret>@<s3 bucket path>.

The following screenshot is an example of a filled form:

3. Click **Save**.

Configuring a virtual index

After the provider, we need a new virtual index. On the **Virtual Indexes** tab, click **New Virtual Index**. Add a unique name, the full S3 path to the logs (optionally, we can use **Whitelist** if there are many log types in that path), and then click **Save**:

Setting up a provider and virtual index in the configuration file

We can connect Hunk instances via SSH using our key pair and set up a data provider via configuration files. For a step-by-step guide, see: http://docs.splunk.com/Documentation/Hunk/latest/Hunk/Setupavirtualindex.

In order to connect the instance via the Terminal, we can use the following command:

```
ssh -i <private key> ec2-user@<public DNS>
```

Exploring data

When we have successfully created a virtual index, we can start to explore the data:

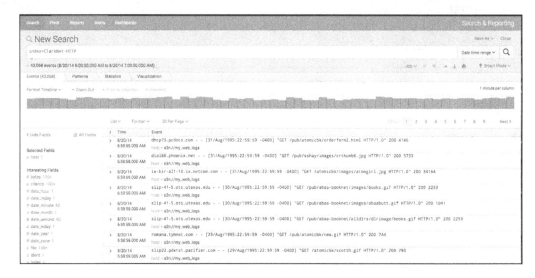

Using SPL we can create reports, depending on what you fancy or want.

Method 2: Hunk–hourly pricing

If we don't have a Hunk license, we can use Hunk on a pay-as-you-go basis. In order to use this method, we should add Hunk as an additional application during the configuration of EMR clusters (see the *Setting up an Amazon EMR cluster* section).

In addition, we have two options for provisioning Hunk.

Provisioning a Hunk instance using the Cloud formation template

We can go to `http://aws.amazon.com/cloudformation/` and create a new stack. Then, we should configure Hunk as usual.

Provisioning a Hunk instance using the EC2 Console

Another option is reusing the EC2 instance. We should find our favorite Hunk AMI and run it. When the cluster is ready, we can create a virtual index that points to a data set location of our choice (HDFS or S3).

Converting Hunk from an hourly rate to a license

We have the option to convert hourly Hunk to a normal license. If we have bought a license, we can add it in **Settings | License | Add License**. Then, we should clear the cache using the following command in the Terminal:

```
rm -rf /opt/hunk/var/run/splunk/hunk/aws/emr/
```

Summary

In this chapter we met Amazon EMR and S3, discussed their advantages for big data analytics and figured out why Hunk is very useful as an analytical tool for cloud Hadoop. In addition, we considered both methods of Hunk licensing in the cloud and learned how to set up EMR clusters and the Hunk AMI. Moreover, we created a new data provider and virtual index based on S3 buckets with access_combined logs. As a result, the reader can solve any big data challenge using cloud computing and avoid the complexity of Hadoop maintenance and deployment.

Index

Thank you for buying
Learning Hunk

About Packt Publishing

Packt, pronounced 'packed', published its first book, *Mastering phpMyAdmin for Effective MySQL Management*, in April 2004, and subsequently continued to specialize in publishing highly focused books on specific technologies and solutions.

Our books and publications share the experiences of your fellow IT professionals in adapting and customizing today's systems, applications, and frameworks. Our solution-based books give you the knowledge and power to customize the software and technologies you're using to get the job done. Packt books are more specific and less general than the IT books you have seen in the past. Our unique business model allows us to bring you more focused information, giving you more of what you need to know, and less of what you don't.

Packt is a modern yet unique publishing company that focuses on producing quality, cutting-edge books for communities of developers, administrators, and newbies alike. For more information, please visit our website at www.packtpub.com.

Writing for Packt

We welcome all inquiries from people who are interested in authoring. Book proposals should be sent to author@packtpub.com. If your book idea is still at an early stage and you would like to discuss it first before writing a formal book proposal, then please contact us; one of our commissioning editors will get in touch with you.

We're not just looking for published authors; if you have strong technical skills but no writing experience, our experienced editors can help you develop a writing career, or simply get some additional reward for your expertise.

Implementing Splunk: Big Data Reporting and Development for Operational Intelligence

ISBN: 978-1-84969-328-8   Paperback: 448 pages

Learn to transform your machine data into valuable IT and business insights with this comprehensive and practical tutorial

1. Learn to search, dashboard, configure, and deploy Splunk on one machine or thousands.

2. Start working with Splunk fast with a tested set of practical examples and useful advice.

3. Step-by-step instructions and examples with a comprehensive coverage for Splunk veterans and newbies alike.

Splunk Operational Intelligence Cookbook

ISBN: 978-1-84969-784-2   Paperback: 414 pages

Over 70 practical recipes to gain operational data intelligence with Splunk Enterprise

1. Learn how to use Splunk to effectively gather, analyze, and report on the operational data across your environment.

2. Expedite your operational intelligence reporting, be empowered to present data in a meaningful way, and shorten the Splunk learning curve.

3. Easy-to-use recipes to help you create robust searches, reports, and charts using Splunk.

Please check **www.PacktPub.com** for information on our titles